Friendship Brace

Friendship
Bracelets

Véronique Follet

Search Press

First published in Great Britain 1995
Search Press Limited
Wellwood, North Farm Road
Tunbridge Wells, Kent TN2 3DR

Reprinted 2000

Originally published in French by Le Temps Apprivoisé,
7, rue Abel-Hovelacque, 75013 Paris, France.
Copyright © 1994 Pierre Zech Editeur, Paris, France.

Photographs copyright © 1995 Search Press Studios except those on pages 1, 3, 5, 6, 7(left), 13, 15, 19, 25, 29, 38, 41, 46, 49, 56, 57, 59 and 60, which are by Janine Sicart, and the margin photographs of the completed bracelets which are by Jean-Loïc Delbord Studios.

The Publishers would like to thank Coats Crafts UK for the supply of the Anchor threads used to test the designs in this book.

ISBN 85532 803 7

Printed in Spain by A. G. Elkar S Coop, 48012 Bilbao

Contents

Introduction

Friendship is universal: it crosses continents, generations and all other barriers...friendship bracelets are for young and old, for teenagers and grandparents, from friend to friend or from boy to girl.

Make a bracelet from colourful threads and tie it on your friend's wrist – he or she will not be able to fasten it without your help – a lasting token of regard and af-fection from one person to another. The bracelets are said to be lucky – the person receiving one makes a wish as the bracelet is fastened on his or her wrist. Then the bracelet should be worn without being removed until it falls off of its own accord when the threads eventually wear out. At that moment, legend has it, the wish will come true.

Friendship bracelets originally came from South and Central America – Chile, Peru, Guatemala, Brazil and other countries – and the names I have given the different bracelets in this book are the names of various towns in those parts of the world.

You will not need any sort of weaving equipment to make these pretty bracelets – they are made simply from a succession of double knots using coloured threads. The only equipment you will need is a safety pin and a pair of scissors!

This is all you do: take several threads (how many you will need depends on which bracelet you have chosen to make), fold them in two and and tie a knot in the folded end to make a loop. Thread an ordinary safety-pin through the loop and then fix it to an anchor point – to your jeans, for example – to keep the threads taut, and you are on your way!

Simple and precise step-by-step instructions show you how to make a wide variety of different bracelets. At the start of each design you will find a brief description of the pattern, my suggestions for colours, and the lengths of thread required to make a bracelet about 15cm (6in) long. The diagrams and the patterns are annotated with an initial letter (corresponding to the colour) and a numeral that indicates the start position of the thread.

All the bracelets are made using two basic knots: forward knots and backward knots. These are described on page 8.

• Forward knots are represented by the symbol →.

• Backward knots are represented by the symbol ←.

Pass a safety pin through the loop and attach the pin and threads to an anchor point.

If you would like to make a bracelet with colours different from those of the model, do not hesitate to copy out the instructions again, simply replacing the initials of the colours used in the model with the initials of the colours you have chosen to use.

When you have mastered the basic technique you could try developing your own designs; include some beadwork, for example, or design a pattern that incorporates a name or some initials.

I recommend that you use a good quality No. 5 pearl cotton thread, which you can get in any sewing shop. You could equally well use No. 3 thread: this is thicker and hence easier to work with when you are starting out. If you do use thicker threads the knots will be bigger, the motif will be wider and you will need to use a longer length of thread to make a bracelet 15cm (6in) long.

The first pattern gives very detailed instructions, knot by knot, to help you learn the basic knots. The degree of detail gets less as you work through the designs but in each case you are given a complete pattern of knots that ends with the colours back in the same order as at the start.

Basic knots

All the designs in this book are made using two basic knots: the forward knot and the backward knot. Each knot is made from two simple loops and the construction for each is described and illustrated below. Do practise the knots before trying to make a bracelet.

To keep your work even it is important to pull the second loop firmly up against the first and to tie subsequent knots tight against each other.

In general the relative position of each of the knots in the first row of a design will affect the look of the finished bracelet, so ensure that you take care at the start.

Preparing the threads

Cut three equal lengths of different coloured threads. Fold all the threads in half and tie a knot in the folded end to give six working threads. For this demonstration I have used green (G1 and G6), orange (O2 and O5) and yellow (Y3 and Y4). Fix a safety pin through the loop formed by the knot and arrange the threads as shown below. Alternatively, you could work on a flat surface and fix the knotted end of the threads to the surface with some adhesive tape.

Forward knot

The instructions below involve making a forward knot with the left-hand green thread (G1) around the orange thread (O2). Note that at the completion of the knot the threads change places.

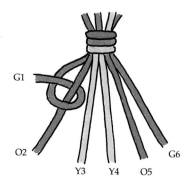

1. Hold thread O2 taut in your left hand and pass thread G1 over and then under thread P2 to form the first loop.

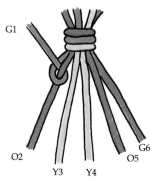

2. Keeping O2 taut, pull G1 upwards to the left to tighten the first loop.

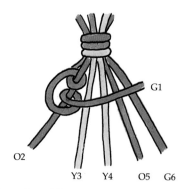

3. Still keeping O2 taut, pass thread G1 over and under O2 once more, pulling it to the right, to make the second loop.

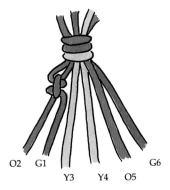

4. Holding O2 taut, pull thread G1 to tighten the second loop against the first and create a forward knot.

Backward knot

These instructions involve making a backward knot with the right-hand green thread (G6) around the orange thread (O5). Note that at the completion of the knot the threads change places.

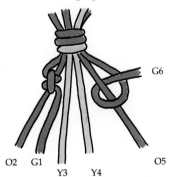

1. Hold the thread O5 taut in your left hand and pass thread G6 over and then under thread O5 to form the first loop.

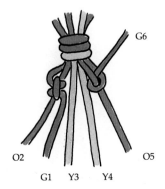

2. Keeping O5 taut, pull G6 upwards to the right to tighten the first loop.

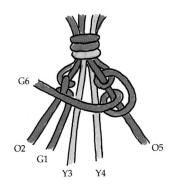

3. Still keeping O5 taut, pass thread G6 over and under O5 once more, pulling it to the left, to make the second loop.

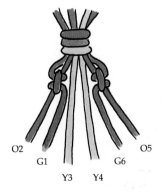

4. Holding O5 taut, pull thread G6 to tighten the second loop against the first and create a backward knot.

Taisha

This is a simple bracelet to start you off. Four different coloured threads are used to create a chevron pattern that repeats every four rows. Before beginning the bracelet, do practise the basic forward and backward knots shown on pages 8 and 9.

You will need four 1.5m (60in) lengths of thread. For this exercise I have used **pink** *(P1 and P8),* **yellow** *(Y2 and Y7),* **violet** *(V3 and V6) and* **green** *(G4 and G5).*

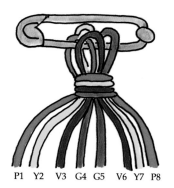

P1 Y2 V3 G4 G5 V6 Y7 P8

Fold the threads in half and tie a simple knot. Pass a safety pin through the loop and use the pin to hold the threads while you work on the bracelet. Separate the threads into the order shown above.

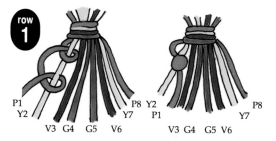

P1 → Y2

1a. Start at the left-hand side and make a forward knot with thread P1 around Y2.

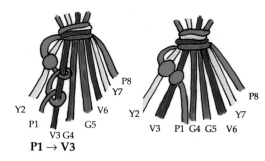

P1 → V3

1b. Make a forward knot with thread P1 around V3, pulling it tight against the first knot.

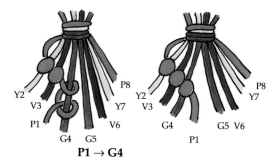

P1 → G4

1c. Now make two forward loops of thread P1 around G4 and make a third forward knot to complete one half of the row.

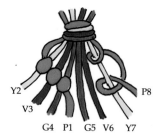

Y7 ← P8

1d. Move to the right-hand side and make a backward knot with thread P8 around Y7.

10

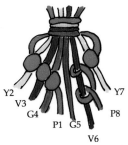

$$V6 \leftarrow P8$$

1e. Make a backward knot with thread P8 around V6 and pull it tight against the first one.

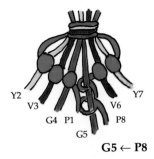

$$G5 \leftarrow P8$$

1f. Make a backward knot with thread P8 around G5 and pull it tight against the others to form the second half-row.

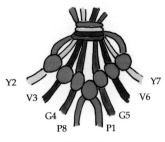

$$P1 \rightarrow P8$$

1g. Make a forward knot with thread P1 around P8 and pull it tight to complete the first row. Adjust the position of the knots to form a good even V-shape of pink knots.

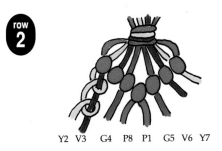

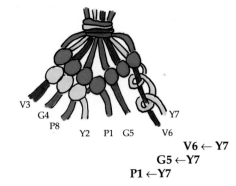

$$Y2 \rightarrow V3$$
$$Y2 \rightarrow G4$$
$$Y2 \rightarrow P8$$

2a. Start the second row at the left-hand side and make forward knots with thread Y2 around V3, then G4 and finally P8, pulling each knot up against the pink knots in the first row.

$$V6 \leftarrow Y7$$
$$G5 \leftarrow Y7$$
$$P1 \leftarrow Y7$$

2b. Move to the right-hand side and make two backward knots with thread Y7 around V6, then G5 and finally P1, pulling each knot up against the pink knots in the first row.

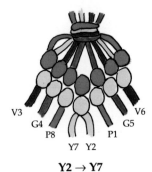

$$Y2 \rightarrow Y7$$

2c. Make a forward knot with thread Y2 around Y7 and pull it tight to complete the second row. Adjust the position of the knots to form a good even V-shape of yellow knots.

row 3

V3 → G4   G5 ← V6
   V3 → P8   P1 ← V6
      V3 → Y7   Y2 ← V6
         V3 → V6

The order of threads at the end of this row is:
   G4, P8, Y7, V6, V3, Y2, P1, G5

row 4

G4 → P8   P1 ← G5
   G4 → Y7   Y2 ← G5
      G4 → V6   V3 ← G5
         G4 → G5

The order of threads at the end of this row is:
   P8, Y7, V6, G5, G4, V3, Y2, P1

rows 5–8

P8 → Y7   Y2 ← P1
   P8 → V6   V3 ← P1
      P8 → G5   G4 ← P1
Y7 → V6   P8 → P1   V3 ← Y2
   Y7 → G5   G4 ← Y2
      Y7 → P1   P8 ← Y2
V6 → G5   Y7 → Y2   G4 ← V3
   V6 → P1   P8 ← V3
      V6 →Y2   Y7 ← V3
G5 → P1   V6 → V3   P8 ← G4
   G5 → Y2   Y7 ← G4
      G5 → V3   V6 ← G4
         G5 → G4

At the end of the eighth row the chevron pattern has been repeated twice and the threads are in the same order as at the beginning:
   P1, Y2, V3, G4, G5, V6, Y7, P8

Completing the bracelet

Continue making rows of different coloured knots until you have reached the required length. Finish the bracelet by separating the threads into two groups of four; plait a short length of each group and tie off each with a small knot.

When the bracelet is long enough, separate the threads into two groups, plait a short length of each, and tie off the ends with small knots.

A selection of the designs that can be found in this book. From left to right: Tarata, Bisinaca, Izalco, Caguán, Yanayacu, Recife, Taisha, Azapa, Amaluza and Abunai.

Jipijapa

This bracelet is straight-sided and has an inverted-V design down its entire length. Three colours are used: one creates a full V-shape across the width and the other two provide alternating blocks of colour. It is important to position the first row of knots to give the inverted V-shape.

You will need two 1.7m (67in) lengths each of a green thread (G1–G4) and a blue thread (B7–B10) and one 1.6m (63in) length of an orange thread (O5 and O6)..

G1 G2 G3 G4 O5 O6 B7 B8 B9 B10

Fold the threads in half, tie a knot and attach a safety pin to hold the threads while you work on the bracelet. Separate the threads into the order shown above.

row 1

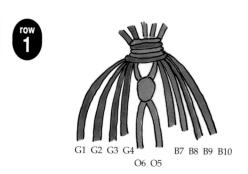

G1 G2 G3 G4   B7 B8 B9 B10
O6 O5

O5 → O6

1a. Start with the middle threads O5 and O6 and make a forward knot with O5 around O6. The threads change places.

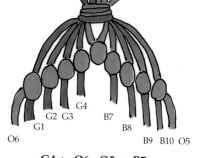

G4
G2 G3   B7
G1   B8
O6   B9 B10 O5

G4 ← O6   O5 → B7
G3 ← O6   O5 → B8
G2 ← O6   O5 → B9
G1 ← O6   O5 → B10

1b. Working towards the left, make a half-row of backward knots with O6 around threads G4, G3, G2 and G1, pulling them tight against each other. Move back to the centre and, working to the right, make a half-row of forward knots with thread O5 around B7, B8, B9 and B10.

row 2

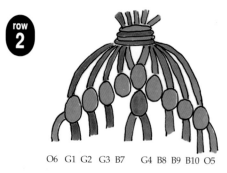

O6   G1   G2   G3   B7   G4   B8   B9   B10   O5

G4 → B7

2a. Return to the middle and make a forward knot with G4 around B7.

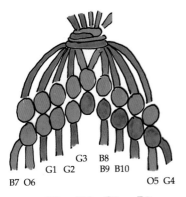

G3　B8
G1　G2　　B9　B10
B7　O6　　　　　　　　O5　G4

$$G3 \leftarrow B7 \quad G4 \rightarrow B8$$
$$G2 \leftarrow B7 \qquad G4 \rightarrow B9$$
$$G1 \leftarrow B7 \qquad\quad G4 \rightarrow B10$$
$$O6 \leftarrow B7 \qquad\qquad G4 \rightarrow O5$$

2b. Working towards the left, make a half-row of backward knots with B7 around G3, G2, G1 and O6, pulling them tight against each other. Move back to the centre and, working to the right, make a half-row of forward knots with thread G4 around B8, B9, B10 and O5.

rows 3–5

B7　O6　O5　G4
B10　B9　B8　　　　　　　G3　G2　G1

$$G3 \rightarrow B8$$
$$G2 \leftarrow B8 \quad G3 \rightarrow B9$$
$$G1 \leftarrow B8 \qquad\quad G3 \rightarrow B10$$
$$O6 \leftarrow B8 \quad G2 \rightarrow B9 \qquad G3 \rightarrow O5$$
$$B7 \leftarrow B8 \quad G1 \leftarrow B9 \quad G2 \rightarrow B10 \qquad G3 \rightarrow G4$$
$$O6 \leftarrow B9 \qquad\quad G2 \rightarrow O5$$
$$B7 \leftarrow B9 \quad G1 \rightarrow B10 \qquad G2 \rightarrow G4$$
$$B8 \leftarrow B9 \quad O6 \leftarrow B10 \quad G1 \rightarrow O5 \quad G2 \rightarrow G3$$
$$B7 \leftarrow B10 \qquad\quad G1 \rightarrow G4$$
$$B8 \leftarrow B10 \qquad\qquad G1 \rightarrow G3$$
$$B9 \leftarrow B10 \qquad\qquad\quad G1 \rightarrow G2$$

Repeat three more rows of blue and green knots, using the pattern above. At the end of the fifth row the threads are in the reverse order to that at the start, and you have completed the first segment of the pattern.

Completing the bracelet

Repeat the design from the first row, using the threads in the order shown above. After a further five rows the threads will be arranged in the same order as they were at the beginning. Now continue adding more segments until the bracelet is the required length.

Finish the bracelet by plaiting threads 1 to 3, 4 to 7 and 8 to 10 and then tying the ends with three small knots.

From left to right: Taisha, Ocotal, Chinajá, Amaluza, Tarata, Tucanao, Azapa, and Jipijapa.

15

Amaluza

This pattern is based on a chevron design but alternate rows of knots are raised above the others. To achieve this effect a slightly different method is used. In the first row and all odd-numbered rows, the thread making a forward knot is moved back to the left, and the one making a backward knot is moved back to the right. In the second row and all even-numbered rows the thread making the knot changes over as normal.

*You will need two 1.7m (67in) lengths each of five different coloured threads. The colours used here are **magenta** (M1 and M10), **pink** (P2 and P9), **violet** (V3 and V8), **fuchsia** (F4 and F7) and **yellow** (Y5 and Y6).*

M1 P2 V3 F4 Y5 Y6 F7 V8 P9 M10

Fold the threads in half, tie a knot and fix a safety pin through the loop. Separate the threads into the order shown above.

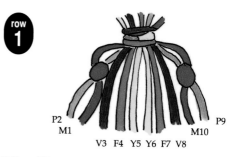

row 1

M1 → P2   **P9 ← M10**

1a. Start with the outside threads and make a forward knot with M1 around P2 and a backward knot with M10 around P9.

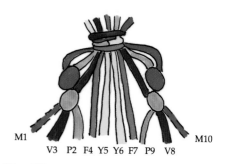

P2 → V3   **V8 ← P9**

1b. Move M1 back one thread to the left and M10 back one thread to the right. Now make a forward knot with P2 around V3 and a backward knot with P9 around V8.

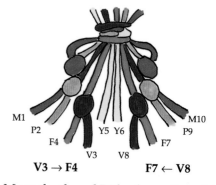

V3 → F4   **F7 ← V8**

1c. Move the thread P2 back one thread to the left and P9 one thread to the right. Now make a forward knot with V3 around F4 and a backward knot with V8 around F7.

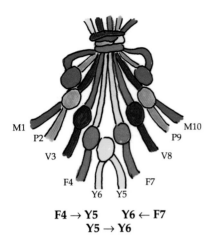

$$F4 \rightarrow Y5 \qquad Y6 \leftarrow F7$$
$$Y5 \rightarrow Y6$$

1d. Move the thread V3 back one thread to the left and V8 one thread to the right. Now make a forward knot with F4 around Y5 and a backward knot with F7 around Y6. Move the fuchsia threads back one thread and complete the row by making a forward knot with Y5 around Y6; allow these threads to change over.

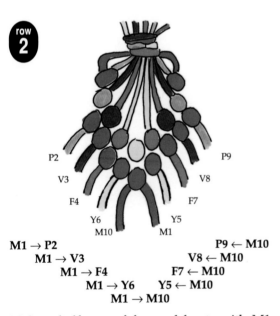

$$M1 \rightarrow P2 \qquad P9 \leftarrow M10$$
$$M1 \rightarrow V3 \qquad V8 \leftarrow M10$$
$$M1 \rightarrow F4 \qquad F7 \leftarrow M10$$
$$M1 \rightarrow Y6 \qquad Y5 \leftarrow M10$$
$$M1 \rightarrow M10$$

Make a half row of forward knots with M1 around threads P2, V3, F4 and Y6 and a row of backward knots with M10 around threads P9, V8, F7, and Y5. Make a forward knot with M1 around M10 to complete the V-shape, which should appear raised above the previous row.

row 3

$$P2 \rightarrow V3 \qquad\qquad V8 \leftarrow P9$$
$$V3 \rightarrow F4 \qquad\qquad F7 \leftarrow V8$$
$$F4 \rightarrow Y6 \qquad\qquad Y5 \leftarrow F7$$
$$Y6 \rightarrow M10 \qquad M1 \leftarrow Y5$$
$$M10 \rightarrow M1$$

Refer to stages 1a to 1b of the first-row instructions and make a series of forward and backward knots, moving the threads back to the left and right respectively. Complete the chevron by making a forward knot with M10 around M1, allow the threads to change places.

row 4

$$P2 \rightarrow V3 \qquad\qquad V8 \leftarrow P9$$
$$P2 \rightarrow F4 \qquad\qquad F7 \leftarrow P9$$
$$P2 \rightarrow Y6 \qquad\qquad Y5 \leftarrow P9$$
$$P2 \rightarrow M1 \qquad M10 \leftarrow P9$$
$$P2 \rightarrow P9$$

Refer to the instructions for the second row but use threads P2 and P9 to make the knots of another raised V-shape. At the end of the row the order of the threads is:

V3, F4, Y6, M1, P9, P2, M10, Y5, F7, V8.

Completing the bracelet

Continue the design, working the odd-numbered rows as for the pattern for the first row and the even-numbered rows as for the second row. As the design develops, you will notice how the sequence of raised rows of solid colour repeats in the order magenta, pink, violet, fuchsia and yellow. When you have made the bracelet long enough, finish it off by plaiting the threads in groups (1–3, 4–7 and 8–10).

Yanayacu

This design is a little more complicated than the earlier ones and is fairly loose in construction. A pattern of small Vs repeats down the middle of the bracelet and is surrounded by a multi-coloured border. The 'rows' of knots are actually tied in layers rather than straight rows, and after four layers of knots the colour pattern is complete but the order of threads is reversed. After eight layers the order of threads returns to that at the beginning.

*You will need 1.6m (63in) lengths of four different coloured threads. I have used **red** (R1 and R8), **yellow** (Y2 and Y7), **green** (G3 and G6) and **violet** (V4 and V5).*

R1 Y2 G3 V4   V5 G6 Y7 R8

Fold the threads in half, tie a knot and attach a safety pin. Separate the threads into the order shown above.

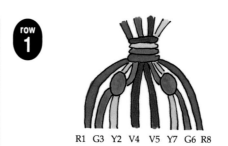

row 1

R1 G3 Y2 V4 V5 Y7 G6 R8

Y2 ← G3   **G6 → Y7**

1a. On the left-hand side, move threads R1 and V4 aside and make a backward knot with G3 around Y2. On the right-hand side, move threads V5 and R8 aside and make a forward knot with G6 around Y7.

G3 R1 Y2 V4 V5 Y7 R8 G6

R1 → G3   **G6 ← R8**

1b. Now make a forward knot with R1 around G3 and a backward knot with R8 around G6.

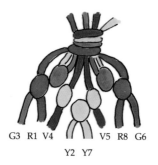

G3 R1 V4   V5 R8 G6
Y2 Y7

Y2 → V4   **V5 ← Y7**
Y2 → Y7

1c. Again, ignore the threads G3 and R1 on the left-hand side and make a forward knot with Y2 around V4. On the right-hand side, ignore G6 and R8 and make a backward knot with Y7 around V5. Complete the layer by making a forward knot with Y2 around Y7. Note how the yellow threads form a small V.

18

row 2

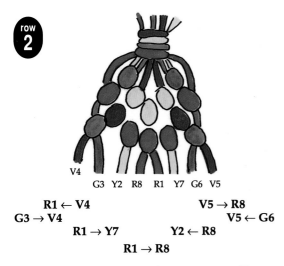

V4

G3 Y2 R8 R1 Y7 G6 V5

R1 ← V4		V5 → R8
G3 → V4		V5 ← G6
R1 → Y7	Y2 → R8	
	R1 → R8	

Work this layer in a similar sequence of knots to that described above and end with a small red V-shape.

rows 3–4

G3 ← Y7		Y2 → G6
V4 → Y7		Y2 ← V5
G3 → R8	R1 ← G6	
	G3 → G6	
V4 ← R8		R1 → V5
Y7 → R8		R1 ← Y2
V4 → G6	G3 ← V5	
	V4 → V5	

Work the third and fourth layers using the sequence of knots shown above to create a small green V-shape followed by a violet one. The order of threads at the end of this row is the reverse of that at the beginning.

Completing the bracelet

Use the pattern given for rows 1 to 4 to continue the design until the bracelet is the required length. Finish by plaiting two groups of threads and tying them off with two knots.

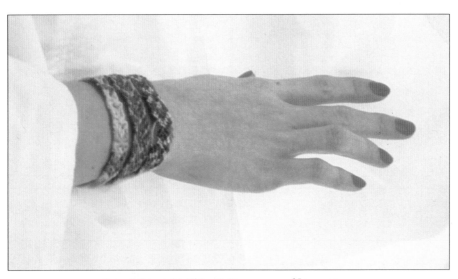

From left to right: Chinajá, Yanayacu and Leguana.

Iquitos

This pretty bracelet needs a little practice to achieve a neat finish. The design creates a series of small V-shapes enclosed within a continuous diamond pattern. It is very important to keep those threads around which the knots are made very tight and to hold them parallel to the length of the bracelet. You must also take care to place the knots accurately.

*You will need three 1.5m (60in) lengths of three colours and one 2m (78in) length of a fourth colour. I have used **fuchsia** (F1 and F8), **blue** (B2 and B7) and **violet** (V3 and V6) for the short threads and **green** (G4 and G5) for the longer one.*

F1 B2 V3 G4   G5 V6 B7 F8

Fold the threads in half, tie a knot in them and attach the knot to a safety pin. Arrange the threads in two groups as shown above.

row 1

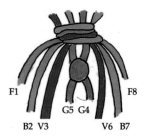

G4 → G5

Start in the middle and make a forward knot with thread G4 around G5.

row 2

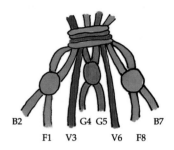

F1 ← B2   **B7 → F8**

Move the outer threads and make a backward knot with B2 around F1 and a forward knot with B7 around F8.

row 3

V3 B2 F1 G4   G5 F8 B7 V6

F1 ← V3   **V6 → F8**
B2 ← V3   **V6 → B7**

Now tie two purple knots on each side, using backward knots with V3 around F1 and B2 and forward knots with V6 around F8 and B7.

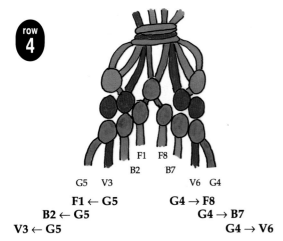

row 4

F1 F8
B2 B7

G5 V3   V6 G4

F1 ← G5   G4 → F8
B2 ← G5   G4 → B7
V3 ← G5   G4 → V6

Create an inverted V-shape by making backward knots with G5 around F1, B2 and V3 and forward knots with G4 around F8, B7 and V6.

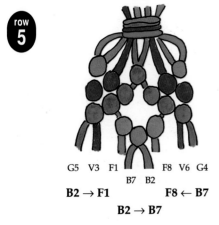

row 5

G5 V3 F1   F8 V6 G4
        B7 B2

B2 → F1   F8 ← B7
        B2 → B7

Make a forward knot with B2 around F1, a back-ward knot with B7 around F8, and then a forward knot with B2 around B7 to give a small V-shape.

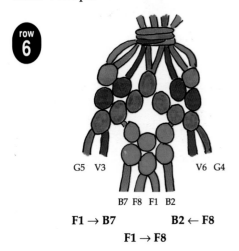

row 6

G5 V3   V6 G4

B7 F8 F1 B2

F1 → B7   B2 ← F8
        F1 → F8

Now create another small V-shape using threads F1 and F8.

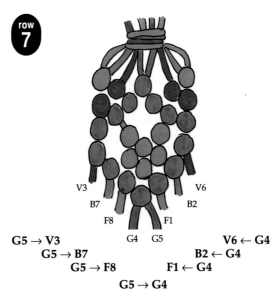

row 7

V3   V6
    B7   B2
        F8   F1
            G4 G5

G5 → V3   V6 ← G4
    G5 → B7   B2 ← G4
        G5 → F8   F1 ← G4
            G5 → G4

Make a full row of green using forward knots of G5 and backward knots of G4 to complete the diamond pattern. The last knot is actually the same knot in the pattern as that in row 1 but with the threads changed over. The shape of the design has now been developed.

rows 8–13

V3 ← B7   B2 → V6
    V3 ← F8   F1 → V6
B7 ← F8   F1 → B2
        V3 ← G4   G5 → V6
    B7 ← G4   G5 → B2
F8 ← G4   G5 → F1
        B7 → V3   V6 ← B2
            B7 → B2
        V3 → B2   B7 ← V6
            V3 → V6
G4 → F8   F1 ← G5
    G4 → B2   B7 ← G5
        G4 → V6   V3 ← G5
            G4 → G5

Follow the pattern to develop the complete colour design. In this diamond shape the small V-shapes will be blue and violet.

Completing the bracelet

At the end of row 13 the colour order of the threads is the same as at the start, although the numerical order is not. Continue by repeating rows 2–13. When the bracelet is long enough, finish by plaiting two groups of threads and tying them off with two small knots.

Bagazán

This is another bracelet that requires a little practice in the placing of the knots. The sequence of knots produces a series of arrow-heads, all in one colour, which are separated by a series of three simple chevrons in alternating colours.

*You will need three 1.6m (63in) lengths of coloured threads and one 2m (78in) length of a fourth colour. In this example I have used **pink** (P1 and P8), **red** (R3 and R6) and **green** (G4 and G5) for the shorter threads and **magenta** (M2 and M7) for the longer one.*

P1 M2 R3 G4 G5 R6 M7 P8

As usual, fold the threads in half, make a small knot in the folded end and fix to a safety pin. Arrange the threads in the order shown in the diagram above.

row 1

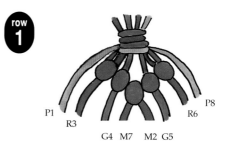

P1 R3   G4 M7 M2 G5   R6 P8

M2 → R3   R6 ← M7
 M2 → G4   G5 ← M7
  M2 → M7

Make a series of forward and backward knots with the threads M2 and M7 to create a V-shape.

row 2

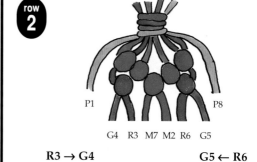

P1   P8

G4 R3 M7 M2 R6 G5

R3 → G4   G5 ← R6

Make a forward and a backward knot with R3 and R6 around G4 and G5 respectively.

row 3

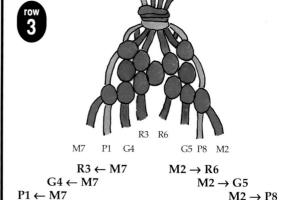

R3 R6
M7 P1 G4   G5 P8 M2

  R3 ← M7   M2 → R6
 G4 ← M7   M2 → G5
P1 ← M7   M2 → P8

Make three backward knots with M7 and three forward knots with M2. Pull the knots into a horizontal line (rather than the usual V-shape) to form the back of the arrowhead.

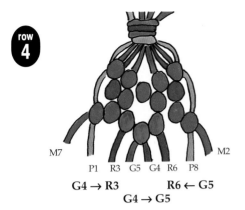

row 4

M7   M2

P1   R3   G5   G4   R6   P8

G4 → R3   R6 ← G5

G4 → G5

Form a small V; make a forward knot with G4 around R3, a backward one with G5 around R6 and a further forward knot with G4 around G5.

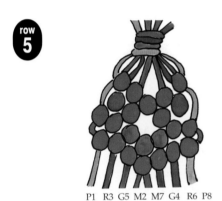

row 5

P1   R3   G5   M2   M7   G4   R6   P8

M7 → P1   P8 ← M2

M7 → R3   R6 ← M2

M7 → G5   G4 ← M2

M7 → M2

Make the arrowhead with forward knots of V7 and backward knots of V2.

row 6

R3   G5   P1   M2   M7   P8   G4   R6

P1 → R3   R6 ← P8

P1 → G5   G4 ← P8

Make two forward knots with P1 and two backward knots with P8.

row 7

G5   P1   M2   R3   R6   M7   P8   G4

R3 → G5   G4 ← R6

R3 → P1   P8 ← R6

R3 → M2   M7 ← R6

Make three forward knots with R3 and three backward knots with R6, following the shape of the previous row again.

row 8

P1   M2   R3   G4   G5   R6   M7   P8   G5

G5 → P1   P8 ← G4

G5 → M2   M7 ← G4

G5 → R3   R6 ← G4

G5 → G4

Finally, make a V-shape series of forward and backward knots with G5 and G4 respectively to complete the pattern.

Completing the bracelet

At the end of row 8 the order of threads is exactly the same as at the beginning. Continue the design by repeating rows 1–8. When the bracelet is long enough, finish by plaiting two groups of threads and tying them off with two small knots.

23

Tarata

Here is another simple bracelet to try. Only backward knots are used in this four-colour design, to create diagonal lines of knots. Each row alternates between four knots of the four chosen colours and seven knots of a single colour. Down the length of the bracelet the rows of solid colour repeat in the same sequence as the order of the threads. You can also make a similar design (with the diagonals in the opposite direction) by working from the left-hand side and using only forward knots.

You will need four 1.6m (63in) lengths of different coloured threads; here I have used **violet** *(V1 and V2),* **blue** *(B3 and B4),* **yellow** *(Y5 and Y6)* *and* **fuchsia** *(F7 and F8).*

V1 V2 B3 B4   Y5 Y6 F7 F8

Fold them in half, tie a knot, attach a safety pin and arrange the threads in the order shown above.

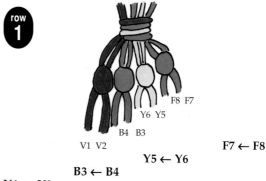

row 1

F8 F7
Y6 Y5
B4 B3
V1 V2
$F7 \leftarrow F8$
$Y5 \leftarrow Y6$
$B3 \leftarrow B4$
$V1 \leftarrow V2$

Start on the right-hand side and make four backward knots with each pair of coloured threads, positioning them as a diagonal line moving down to the left.

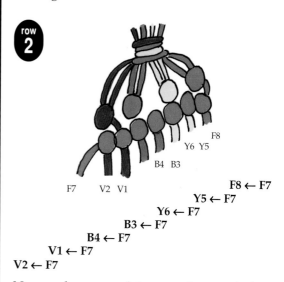

row 2

F8
Y6 Y5
B4 B3
F7   V2 V1
$F8 \leftarrow F7$
$Y5 \leftarrow F7$
$Y6 \leftarrow F7$
$B3 \leftarrow F7$
$B4 \leftarrow F7$
$V1 \leftarrow F7$
$V2 \leftarrow F7$

Now make a complete row of seven fuchsia knots, again starting on the right-hand side.

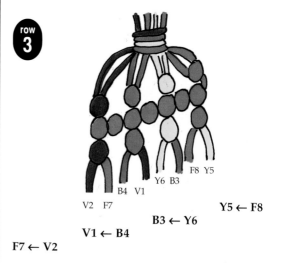

row 3

F8 Y5
Y6 B3
B4 V1
V2 F7
$Y5 \leftarrow F8$
$B3 \leftarrow Y6$
$V1 \leftarrow B4$
$F7 \leftarrow V2$

Make four knots with each pair of threads.

24

row 4

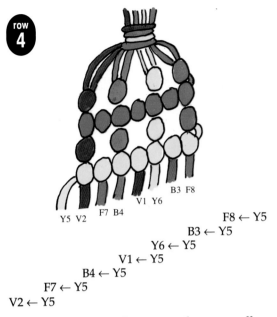

B3 F8

V1 Y6

F7 B4

Y5 V2

F8 ← Y5

B3 ← Y5

Y6 ← Y5

V1 ← Y5

B4 ← Y5

F7 ← Y5

V2 ← Y5

Now make a complete row of seven yellow knots, again starting on the right-hand side.

rows 5–8

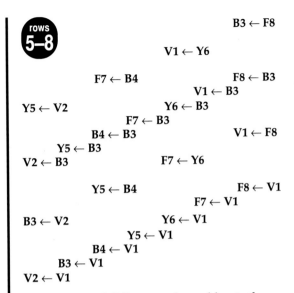

B3 ← F8

V1 ← Y6

F7 ← B4   F8 ← B3

V1 ← B3

Y5 ← V2   Y6 ← B3

F7 ← B3

B4 ← B3   V1 ← F8

Y5 ← B3

V2 ← B3   F7 ← Y6

Y5 ← B4   F8 ← V1

F7 ← V1

B3 ← V2   Y6 ← V1

Y5 ← V1

B4 ← V1

B3 ← V1

V2 ← V1

Make a row of different coloured knots then a row of blue ones. Make another row of different coloured knots and then a row of violet ones to complete the design.

Completing the bracelet

At the end of row 8 the threads are in the same order as at the start. Continue by repeating rows 1–8. Finish by plaiting two groups of threads and tying them off with small knots.

From top to bottom: Itatuba, Tarata and Yanayacu.

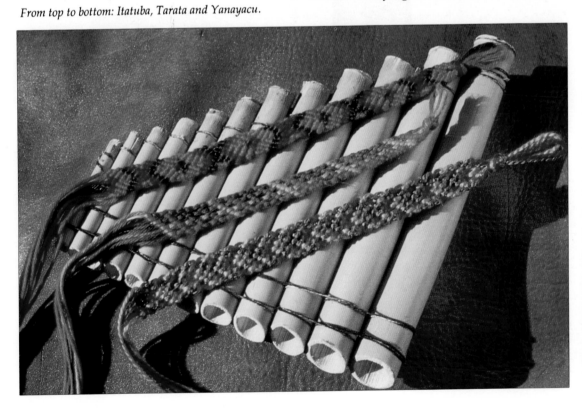

Bisinaca

This is another diagonal design that is made with eight threads in four colours. Again, only backward knots are used, but, as with other diagonal patterns, you could start at the left-hand side and work in reverse using forward knots. This pattern introduces openwork by creating a series of small holes down the length of the bracelet. The pattern repeats every eight rows.

To follow the diagrams of this pattern you will need four 1.6m (63in) lengths of different coloured threads: **red** (R1 and R8), **green** (G2 and G7), **blue** (B3 and B6) and **orange** (O4 and O5).

R1 G2 B3 O4   O5 B6 G7 R8

Fold all the threads in half, form a knot in the folded end, attach a safety pin and arrange the threads in the order shown above.

The bracelet shown in the margin pictures was made with only forward knots – note the change in angle of the diagonal lines.

26

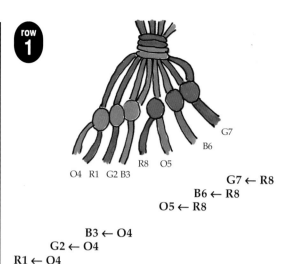

row 1

G7
B6
O4 R1 G2 B3   R8 O5

G7 ← R8
B6 ← R8
O5 ← R8

B3 ← O4
G2 ← O4
R1 ← O4

Working from the right, make three backward knots with R8 around G7, B6 and O5. Now take up thread O4 and make three backward knots around B3, G2 and R1. Slide the knots down the threads to form a neat diagonal line.

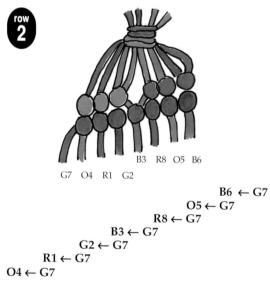

row 2

B3 R8 O5 B6
G7 O4 R1 G2

B6 ← G7
O5 ← G7
R8 ← G7
B3 ← G7
G2 ← G7
R1 ← G7
O4 ← G7

Still working from the right-hand side, make a complete row of seven backward knots with G7, pulling them up tight up against those in the first row.

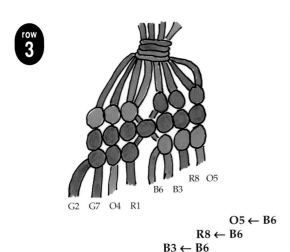

row 3

R8 O5
B6 B3
G2 G7 O4 R1

O5 ← B6
R8 ← B6
B3 ← B6

R1 ← G2
O4 ← G2
G7 ← G2

Repeat the pattern of the first row with threads B6 and G2.

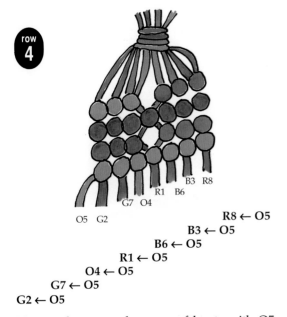

row 4

B3 R8
R1 B6
G7 O4
O5 G2

R8 ← O5
B3 ← O5
B6 ← O5
R1 ← O5
O4 ← O5
G7 ← O5
G2 ← O5

Now make a complete row of knots with O5. Note the small hole that appears in the middle of the bracelet, between the third and fourth rows.

rows 5–8

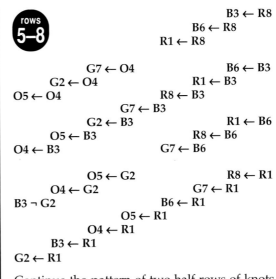

B3 ← R8
B6 ← R8
R1 ← R8

G7 ← O4   B6 ← B3
G2 ← O4   R1 ← B3
O5 ← O4   R8 ← B3
          G7 ← B3
          G2 ← B3   R1 ← B6
          O5 ← B3   R8 ← B6
O4 ← B3   G7 ← B6

          O5 ← G2   R8 ← R1
          O4 ← G2   G7 ← R1
B3 ¬ G2   B6 ← R1
          O5 ← R1
          O4 ← R1
          B3 ← R1
G2 ← R1

Continue the pattern of two half rows of knots made with with R8 and O4, a full row with B3, a further two half rows with B6 and G2, and, finally, make a solid row of red knots with R1 to complete the pattern. The threads are now in the same order as they are at the start.

Completing the bracelet

Continue the design by repeating rows 1–8. When the bracelet is long enough, finish it by plaiting two groups of threads and tying them off with two small knots.

27

Cafifi

This is another openwork-type bracelet using eight threads but just two colours. The four threads down the middle make a continuous arrowhead design while the outer two threads on each side form a contrasting border that has a scalloped edge.

*You will need two 1.5m (60in) lengths of **green** thread (G1, G2, G7 and G8) and two similar lengths of **violet** thread (V3, V4, V5 and V6).*

G1 G2 V3 V4   V5 V6 G7 G8

Fold them in half, make a knot and attach a safety pin. Arrange the threads in the order shown above.

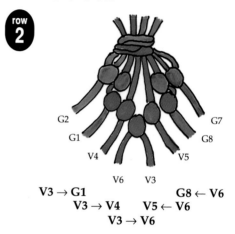

row 1

G2   G7
V3   V6
G1 V4 V5 G8

G1 → G2	G7 ← G8
G1 → V3	V6 ← G8

Make two forward knots with G1 around G2 and V3 and two backward knots with G8 around G7 and V6.

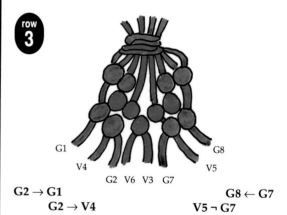

row 2

G2   G7
G1   G8
V4   V5
V6   V3

V3 → G1	G8 ← V6
V3 → V4	V5 ← V6
V3 → V6	

Ignore the outermost threads and form a V-shape by knotting threads V3 and V6 as shown above.

row 3

G1   G8
V4   V5
G2 V6 V3 G7

G2 → G1	G8 ← G7
G2 → V4	V5 ¬ G7

Now make a forward knot with G2 around G1, allowing a short length of G2 to loop round the first violet knot in the row above, then make another forward knot with G2 around V4. In a similar way, make two backward knots with G7 around G8 and V5.

28

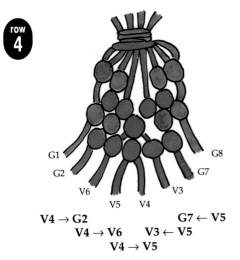

G1 G8
G2 G7
V6 V3
V5 V4

$$V4 \rightarrow G2 \qquad\qquad G7 \leftarrow V5$$
$$V4 \rightarrow V6 \qquad V3 \leftarrow V5$$
$$V4 \rightarrow V5$$

Again, ignore the outermost threads and form a V-shape by knotting threads V4 and V5 as shown above.

Completing the bracelet

At the end of the fourth row the green threads G1, G2, G7 and G8 are in the same position as at the beginning, but although all the violet threads are in the middle, their numerical order is reversed. However, you can continue working the design as for rows 1–4, substituting thread numbers until the bracelet is long enough. Then separate the threads into two groups, plait them and tie them off with two small knots.

From left to right: Iquitos, Chinajá, Leguana, Jipijapa and Mucura.

Caguán

Raised diagonal ridges of solid colour that are separated by a multi-coloured background are created with this pattern. The two rows of background knots are worked slightly differently from previous designs. Normally the thread making the knot changes place with the thread around which the knot is made. However, here the thread making the knot is moved back over to its original position. It sounds rather complicated, but with a little practice you will soon master it.

You will need four 1.7m (67in) lengths of different coloured thread. **Orange** *(O1 and O5),* **red** *(R2 and R6),* **yellow** *(Y3 and Y7) and* **blue** *(B4 and B8) are the colours used in this example.*

O1 R2 Y3 B4   O5 R6 Y7 B8

Fold all the threads in half, make a knot, attach them to a safety pin and arrange the threads in the order shown above.

row 1

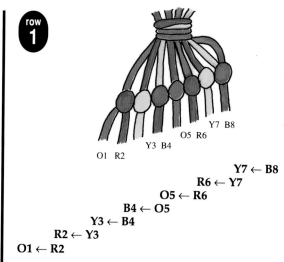

Y7 B8
O5 R6
Y3 B4
O1 R2

Y7 ← B8
R6 ← Y7
O5 ← R6
B4 ← O5
Y3 ← B4
R2 ← Y3
O1 ← R2

Work from the right-hand side and make a backward knot with B8 around Y7. Move B8 back over Y7 and then make a backward knot with Y7 around R6. Move Y7 back over R6 and then continue to make backward knots in a similar way with R6, O5, B4, Y3 and R2. At the end of this row the threads should still be in the same order as at the start.

row 2

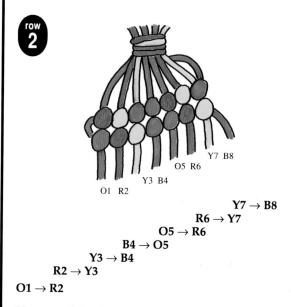

Y7 B8
O5 R6
Y3 B4
O1 R2

Y7 → B8
R6 → Y7
O5 → R6
B4 → O5
Y3 → B4
R2 → Y3
O1 → R2

Now work back up the diagonal from the left, making a row of forward knots. Again, always work with the thread around which the preceding knot is made. At the end of the row the threads will still be in the same order as at the start.

30

row 3

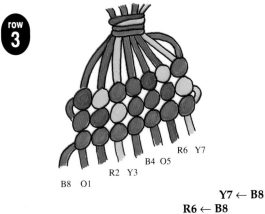

R6 Y7
B4 O5
R2 Y3
B8 O1

Y7 ← B8
R6 ← B8
O5 ← B8
B4 ← B8
Y3 ← B8
R2 ← B8
O1 ← B8

Make a row of backward knots with B8 around Y7, R6, O5, B4, Y3, R2 and O1 to form a solid row of blue knots. In this row the threads change places as normal. This row completes the basic pattern of knots and forms the first raised ridge of the pattern.

rows 4–6

R6 ← Y7
O5 ← R6
B4 ← O5
Y3 ← B4   R6 → Y7
R2 ← Y3   O5 → R6
O1 ← R2   B4 → O5
B8 ← O1   Y3 → B4   R6 ← Y7
R2 → Y3   O5 ← Y7
O1 → R2   B4 ← Y7
B8 → O1   Y3 ← Y7
R2 ← Y7
O1 ← Y7

B8 ← Y7

Start back on the right-hand side, at the top of the diagonal, and make a backward knot with Y7 around R6. Move Y7 back over R6 and then make a backward knot with R6 around O5. Move R6 back over O5 and continue making backward knots in a similar way with O5, B4, Y3, R2 and O1.

Again, work back up the diagonal with a series of forward knots, moving each thread back and then working with the thread around which the previous knot is made.

Complete the second segment of the pattern with a row of backward knots with Y7 around R6, O5, B4, Y3, R2, O1 and B8 to form a solid row of yellow knots and the second raised ridge of the pattern.

rows 7-9

O5 ← R6
B4 ← O5
Y3 ← B4
R2 ← Y3   O5 → R6
O1 ← R2   B4 → O5
B8 ← O1   Y3 → B4
Y7 ← B8   R2 → Y3   O5 ← R6
O1 → R2   B4 ← R6
B8 → O1   Y3 ← R6
Y7 → B8   R2 ← R6
O1 ← R6
B8 ← R6

Y7← R6

These three rows are worked in a similar pattern to that described above and finish with a raised row of red knots.

rows 10–13

B4 ← O5
Y3 ← B4
R2 ← Y3
O1 ← R2   B4 → O5
B8 ← O1   Y3 → B4
Y7 ← B8   R2 → Y3
R6 ←Y7   O1 → R2   B4 ← O5
B8 → O1   Y3 ← O5
Y7 → B8   R2 ← O5
R6 → Y7   O1 ← O5
B8 ← O5
Y7 ← O5

R6 ← O5

At the end of the twelfth row the complete pattern has been developed and it ends with a raised row of orange knots. At this stage the order is:

O5, R6, Y7, B8, O1, R2, Y3 and B4

Completing the bracelet

At the end of the twelfth row the colours are in the same order as at the beginning but the numerical order of the threads will not be the same until the end of the twenty-fourth row. Continue the pattern basically as described for rows one to twelve until the bracelet is at the required length. Separate the threads into two groups of four, plait a short length of each group and tie each off with a small knot.

31

Mucura

This design is a variation of a simple chevron pattern and is made with ten threads in three colours. A series of V-shapes in one colour is enclosed within a border of the other. Each row consists of forward knots from the left-hand side and backward knots from the right. However, in this design the outer two threads on either side always stay on the outside. After the second knot from each side, the thread making the knot is moved back and the row is finished with the thread around which that knot is made.

*You will need two 1.6m (63in) lengths of both **blue** and **green** threads (B1, B2, B6 and B7 and G4, G5, G9 and G10) and a 1.4m (55in) length of **magenta** (M3 and M8).*

B1 B2 M3 G4 G5 B6 B7 M8 G9 G10

Fold all the threads in half, make a knot and attach a safety pin. Arrange the threads in the order shown above.

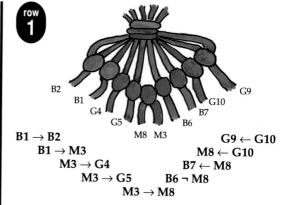

row 1

B2   B1   G10   G9
   G4   G5   M8   B7   B6
     M8   M3

B1 → B2   G9 ← G10
   B1 → M3   M8 ← G10
     M3 → G4   B7 ← M8
       M3 → G5   B6 ¬ M8
         M3 → M8

Make two forward knots with B1 around B2 and M3, and two backward knots with G10 around G9 and M8. Move thread B1 over M3 to the left and thread G10 over M8 to the right, and continue knotting with M3 and M8 to complete the row.

row 2

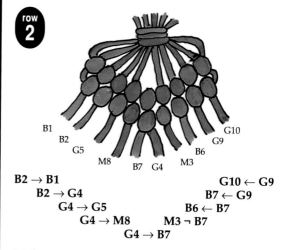

B2 → B1   G10 ← G9
   B2 → G4   B7 ← G9
     G4 → G5   B6 ← B7
       G4 → M8   M3 ¬ B7
         G4 → B7

Make two forward knots with B2 and two backward knots with G9. Move B2 and G9 to the left and right respectively and continue knotting with G4 and B7.

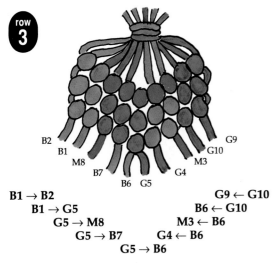

row 3

$B1 \rightarrow B2$
$\quad B1 \rightarrow G5$
$\qquad G5 \rightarrow M8$
$\qquad\quad G5 \rightarrow B7$
$\qquad\qquad G5 \rightarrow B6$

$\hfill G9 \leftarrow G10$
$\hfill B6 \leftarrow G10$
$\hfill M3 \leftarrow B6$
$\hfill G4 \leftarrow B6$

Work this row in a similar way with threads B1, G10, G5 and B6.

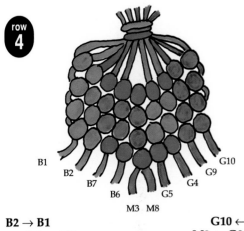

row 4

$B2 \rightarrow B1$
$\quad B2 \rightarrow M8$
$\qquad M8 \rightarrow B7$
$\qquad\quad M8 \rightarrow B6$
$\qquad\qquad M8 \rightarrow M3$

$\hfill G10 \leftarrow G9$
$\hfill M3 \leftarrow G9$
$\hfill G4 \leftarrow M3$
$\hfill G5 \leftarrow M3$

Work this row as above using threads B2, G9, M8 and M3. The magenta knots form a solid V-shape in the middle of the bracelet.

rows 5–6

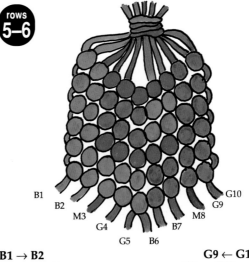

$B1 \rightarrow B2$
$\quad B1 \rightarrow B7$
$\qquad B7 \rightarrow B6$
$\qquad\quad B7 \rightarrow M3 \qquad M8 \leftarrow G4$
$B2 \rightarrow B1 \qquad\qquad B7 \rightarrow G4$
$\quad B2 \rightarrow B6$
$\qquad B6 \rightarrow M3$
$\qquad\quad B6 \rightarrow G4 \qquad B7 \leftarrow G5$
$\qquad\qquad B6 \rightarrow G5$

$\hfill G9 \leftarrow G10$
$\hfill G4 \leftarrow G10$
$\hfill G5 \leftarrow G4$

$\hfill G10 \leftarrow G9$
$\hfill G5 \leftarrow G9$
$\hfill M8 \leftarrow G5$

Continue with two more rows, making knots in the order shown above.

Completing the bracelet

At the end of the sixth row the pattern is complete and the threads are in the same order as they were at the beginning. Repeat the six-row pattern until the bracelet is long enough.

Finally, separate the threads into two groups of five, plait them and tie off the ends with two small knots.

Abunai

The pattern for this bracelet consists of nine diagonal rows of forward knots – with an increasing number of knots in each row – followed by nine rows of backward knots (also with an increasing number of knots in each row) forming a diagonal in the opposite direction. The finished bracelet has a wavy edge down each side and gives the appearance of twisted ribbons.

*You will need 1.6m (63in) lengths of five different coloured threads; this design looks very nice if your colours are of a similar hue. My sample uses **fuchsia** (F1 and F6), **violet** (V2 and V7), **pink** (P3 and P8), **coral** (C4 and C9) and **magenta** (M5 and M10).*

F1 V2 P3 C4 M5 F6 V7 P8 C9 M10

Fold all the threads in half, make a knot, attach a safety pin and arrange the threads as shown above.

---

row 1

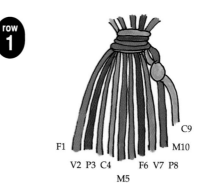

F1   C9   M10
V2 P3 C4   F6 V7 P8
M5

C9 → M10

Ignore the first eight threads from the left and make a forward knot with C9 around M10.

---

row 2

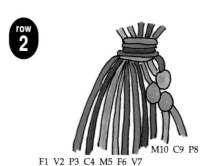

F1 V2 P3 C4 M5 F6 V7   M10 C9 P8

P8 → M10
P8 → C9

Ignore the first seven threads from the left and make two forward knots with P8 around M10 and C9, positioning them as the start of a diagonal line.

---

row 3

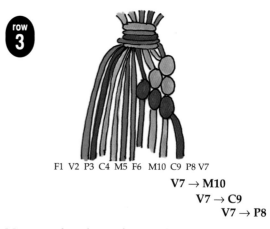

F1 V2 P3 C4 M5 F6   M10 C9 P8 V7

V7 → M10
V7 → C9
V7 → P8

Now make three forward knots with V7 around M10, C9 and P8.

34

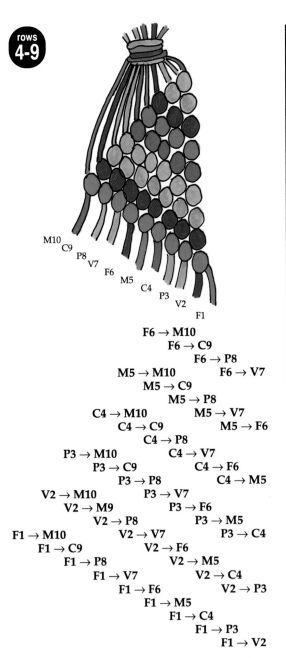

M10 C9 P8 V7 F6 M5 C4 P3 V2 F1

$$F6 \rightarrow M10$$
$$F6 \rightarrow C9$$
$$F6 \rightarrow P8$$
$$M5 \rightarrow M10 \qquad F6 \rightarrow V7$$
$$M5 \rightarrow C9$$
$$M5 \rightarrow P8$$
$$C4 \rightarrow M10 \qquad M5 \rightarrow V7$$
$$C4 \rightarrow C9 \qquad M5 \rightarrow F6$$
$$C4 \rightarrow P8$$
$$P3 \rightarrow M10 \qquad C4 \rightarrow V7$$
$$P3 \rightarrow C9 \qquad C4 \rightarrow F6$$
$$P3 \rightarrow P8 \qquad C4 \rightarrow M5$$
$$V2 \rightarrow M10 \qquad P3 \rightarrow V7$$
$$V2 \rightarrow M9 \qquad P3 \rightarrow F6$$
$$V2 \rightarrow P8 \qquad P3 \rightarrow M5$$
$$F1 \rightarrow M10 \qquad V2 \rightarrow V7 \qquad P3 \rightarrow C4$$
$$F1 \rightarrow C9 \qquad V2 \rightarrow F6$$
$$F1 \rightarrow P8 \qquad V2 \rightarrow M5$$
$$F1 \rightarrow V7 \qquad V2 \rightarrow C4$$
$$F1 \rightarrow F6 \qquad V2 \rightarrow P3$$
$$F1 \rightarrow M5$$
$$F1 \rightarrow C4$$
$$F1 \rightarrow P3$$
$$F1 \rightarrow V2$$

Continue building up the design, making four, five, six, etc., knots with F6, M5, C4, P3, V2 and F1. At the end of the ninth row the colours will be in the reverse order to that at the beginning.

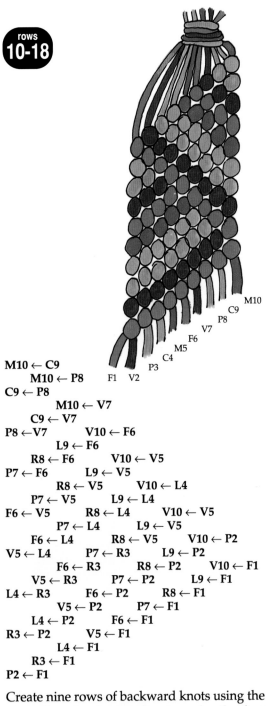

M10 C9 P8 V7 F6 M5 C4 P3 F1 V2

$$M10 \leftarrow C9$$
$$M10 \leftarrow P8$$
$$C9 \leftarrow P8$$
$$M10 \leftarrow V7$$
$$C9 \leftarrow V7$$
$$P8 \leftarrow V7 \qquad V10 \leftarrow F6$$
$$L9 \leftarrow F6$$
$$R8 \leftarrow F6 \qquad V10 \leftarrow V5$$
$$P7 \leftarrow F6 \qquad L9 \leftarrow V5$$
$$R8 \leftarrow V5 \qquad V10 \leftarrow L4$$
$$P7 \leftarrow V5 \qquad L9 \leftarrow L4$$
$$F6 \leftarrow V5 \qquad R8 \leftarrow L4 \qquad V10 \leftarrow V5$$
$$P7 \leftarrow L4 \qquad L9 \leftarrow V5$$
$$F6 \leftarrow L4 \qquad R8 \leftarrow V5 \qquad V10 \leftarrow P2$$
$$V5 \leftarrow L4 \qquad P7 \leftarrow R3 \qquad L9 \leftarrow P2$$
$$F6 \leftarrow R3 \qquad R8 \leftarrow P2 \qquad V10 \leftarrow F1$$
$$V5 \leftarrow R3 \qquad P7 \leftarrow P2 \qquad L9 \leftarrow F1$$
$$L4 \leftarrow R3 \qquad F6 \leftarrow P2 \qquad R8 \leftarrow F1$$
$$V5 \leftarrow P2 \qquad P7 \leftarrow F1$$
$$L4 \leftarrow P2 \qquad F6 \leftarrow F1$$
$$R3 \leftarrow P2 \qquad V5 \leftarrow F1$$
$$L4 \leftarrow F1$$
$$R3 \leftarrow F1$$
$$P2 \leftarrow F1$$

Create nine rows of backward knots using the same thread reference as given for the first nine rows. This set of rows will form diagonals in the opposite direction to the first set.

Completing the bracelet

At the end of the eighteenth row the threads will be in the same order as at the beginning. Continue working the pattern as for rows 1–18 until the bracelet is long enough, then finish off in the usual way.

Itatuba

The three colours used for this bracelet are knotted to form a series of diamonds and crosses. The diamond shapes are the same colour down the length of the bracelet but the centre knots and the crosses alternate between the other two colours. This design looks good when contrasting colours are used.

*To follow the pattern precisely you will need two 1.6m (63in) lengths of **orange** thread (O1, O2, O7 and O8) and one 1.6m length each of **blue** (B3 and B6) and **red** (R4 and R5).*

O1 O2 B3 R4 R5 B6 O7 O8

Fold all the threads in half, make a knot and attach a safety pin. Arrange the threads in the order shown above.

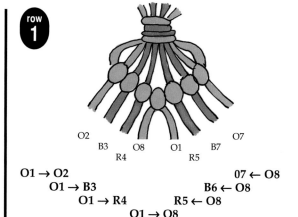

O2   B3   O8   O1   B7
      R4   R5   O7

O1 → O2   07 ← O8
  O1 → B3   B6 ← O8
    O1 → R4   R5 ← O8
      O1 → O8

Make three forward knots with O1 around O2, B3 and R4 and three backward knots with O8 around O7, B6 and R5. Now make a forward knot with O1 around O8 to complete the V-shape. Take care to place each knot correctly.

rows 2-4

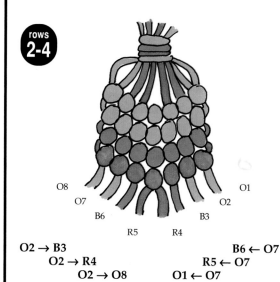

O8   O1
  O7   O2
    B6   B3
        R5   R4

O2 → B3   B6 ← O7
  O2 → R4   R5 ← O7
    O2 → O8   O1 ← O7
      O2 → O7

B3 → R4   R5 ← B6
  B3 → O8   O1 ← B6
    B3 → O7   O2 ← B6
      B3 → B6

R4 → O8   O1 ← R5
  R4 → O7   O2 ← R5
    R4 → B6   B3 ← R5
      R4 → R5

Make three more rows in a similar V-shape with threads O2 and O7, the blue threads B3 and B6 and finally the red ones R4 and R5. Position the knots to keep the V-shape nice and even. At the end of the fourth row the threads are in the reverse order to that at the beginning.

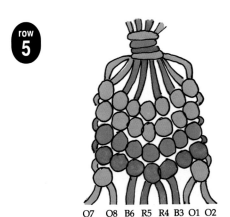

row 5

O7 O8 B6 R5 R4 B3 O1 O2

O8 ← O7   O2 → O1

Tie a backward knot with O7 around O8, placing the knot on the same level as the last red knot. Tie a forward knot with O2 around O1 and place the knot level with the previous knot.

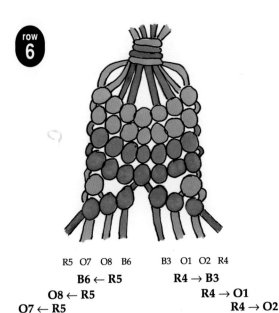

row 6

R5 O7 O8 B6   B3 O1 O2 R4

B6 ← R5   R4 → B3
O8 ← R5   R4 → O1
O7 ← R5   R4 → O2

Make three backward knots with R5 around B6, O8 and O7; place the knots so as to continue the diagonal red line down to the left. Make three forward knots with R4 around B3, O1 and O2 and place the knots so as to complete the red cross.

rows 7-11

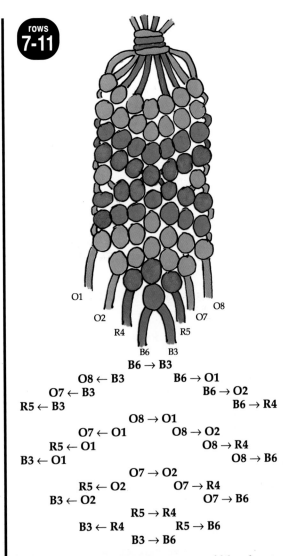

O1   O8

O2   O7

R4   R5

B6   B3

B6 → B3

O8 ← B3   B6 → O1
O7 ← B3   B6 → O2
R5 ← B3   B6 → R4

O8 → O1
O7 ← O1   O8 → O2
R5 ← O1   O8 → R4
B3 ← O1   O8 → B6

O7 → O2
R5 ← O2   O7 → R4
B3 ← O2   O7 → B6

R5 → R4
B3 ← R4   R5 → B6
B3 → B6

Make an inverted V-shape row of blue knots using B3 and B6, working the knots as shown above.

Continue the pattern with a similar row of orange using O1 around O8.

Make a forward knot with O7 around O2 and then make two backward knots with O2 and two forward knots with O7. Do not make the last knot in this row.

Make two forward knots with R5 around R4 and B6 and a backward knot with R4 around B3.

Make a forward knot with B3 around B6 to form an upright V-shape and thus complete the pattern. At the end of this row the orange threads are back in their original positions but the red and blue ones are transposed.

rows 12-22

O1 → O2			O7 ← O8
O1 → R4			R5 ← O8
O1 → B6		B3 ← O8	
	O1 → O8		
O2 → R4			R5 ← O7
O2 → B6		B3 ← O7	
O2 → O8		O1 ← O7	
	O2 → O7		
R4 → B6			B3 ← R5
R4 → O8		O1 ← R5	
R4 → O7		O2 ← R5	
	R4 → R5		
B6 → O8			O1 ← B3
B6 → O7		O2 ← B3	
B6 → R5		R4 ← B3	
	B6 → B3		
O8 ← O7			O2 → O1
R5 ← B3		B6 → R4	
O8 ← B3		B6 → O1	
O7 ← B3			B6 → O2
	R5 → R4		
O8 ← R4		R5 → O1	
O7 ← R4		R5 → O2	
B3 ← R4			R5 → B6
	O8 → O1		
O7 ← O1		O8 → O2	
B3 ← O1		O8 → B6	
R4 ← O1			O8 → R5
	O7 → O2		
B3 ← O2		O7 → B6	
R4 ← O2		O7 → R5	
	B3 → B6		
R4 ← B6		B3 → R5	
	R4 → R5		

Work another eleven row using the series of knots shown above, noting that the red and blue threads are reversed. At the end of the twenty-second rows the colour order of the threads is the same as at the beginning but the numerical order will not be the same until the end of the forty-fourth row.

Completing the bracelet

Repeat the pattern from the beginning until the bracelet is long enough, then tie off the loose ends in the usual way.

Chinajá

Repeating arrowheads are the theme of this design. The pattern is rather difficult to master right away, and you may want to practise with some odd bits of thread. Each arrowhead is made from six rows of knots, which means that the colour pattern only repeats every twenty-four rows. Even so, although the colour order is correct at the end of the twenty-fourth row, the actual order of threads is the reverse of that at the beginning.

*This example is made with shades of green and yellow. You will need four 1.6m (63in) lengths of threads; a **mid green** (G1 and G8), a **yellow** (Y2 and Y7), an **apple green** (A3 and A6) and an **orange** (O4 and O5).*

Prepare the threads as usual and arrange in the order shown above.

row 1

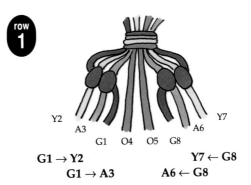

$G1 \rightarrow Y2$ $Y7 \leftarrow G8$
$G1 \rightarrow A3$ $A6 \leftarrow G8$

Make two forward knots with G1 around Y2 and P3, and two backward knots with G8 around Y7 and Y2.

row 2

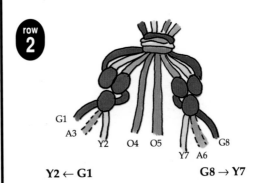

$Y2 \leftarrow G1$ $G8 \rightarrow Y7$

Make a backward knot with G1 around Y2, leaving A3 underneath. Make a forward knot with G8 around Y7, leaving A6 underneath.

row 3

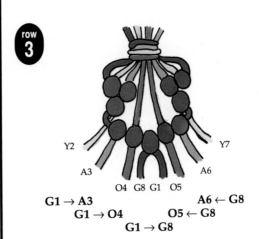

$G1 \rightarrow A3$ $A6 \leftarrow G8$
$G1 \rightarrow O4$ $O5 \leftarrow G8$
$G1 \rightarrow G8$

Move Y2 over A3 to the left and then make two forward knots with G1 around A3 and O4. Move Y7 over A6 to the right and make two backward knots with G8 around A6 and O5. Now make a forward knot with G1 around G8 to complete the back part of the arrowhead. Position the knots to give a neat straight edge on either side.

39

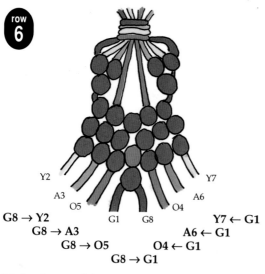

row 4

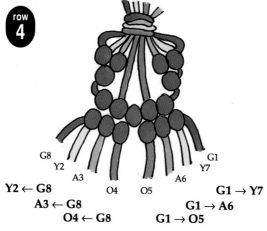

G8
Y2
A3   O4   O5   A6
                   G1
                   Y7

Y2 ← G8   G1 → Y7
    A3 ← G8   G1 → A6
       O4 ← G8   G1 → O5

Work outwards from the middle and make three backward knots with G8 and three forward knots with G1.

row 5

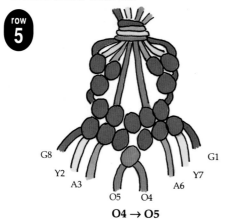

G8   G1
Y2   Y7
   A3   A6
      O5   O4

O4 → O5

In the middle of the bracelet, make a forward knot with O4 around O5.

row 6

Y2   Y7
   A3   A6
     O5   O4

G8 → Y2   G1   G8   Y7 ← G1
   G8 → A3   A6 ← G1
     G8 → O5   O4 ← G1
        G8 → G1

Make forward knots with G8 and backward knots with G1 to complete the first arrowhead.

rows 7-12

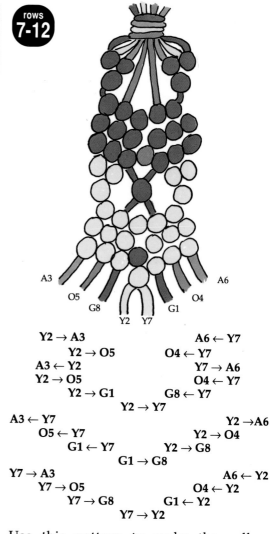

A3   A6
   O5   O4
    G8   G1
      Y2   Y7

Y2 → A3   A6 ← Y7
   Y2 → O5   O4 ← Y7
A3 ← Y2   Y7 → A6
Y2 → O5   O4 ← Y7
   Y2 → G1   G8 ← Y7
       Y2 → Y7

A3 ← Y7   Y2 → A6
   O5 ← Y7   Y2 → O4
     G1 ← Y7   Y2 → G8
       G1 → G8

Y7 → A3   A6 ← Y2
   Y7 → O5   O4 ← Y2
     Y7 → G8   G1 ← Y2
       Y7 → Y2

Use this pattern to make the yellow arrowhead.

rows 13-18

A3 → O5   O4 ← A6
   A3 → G8   G1 ← P6
A3 ← O5   O4 → A6
A3 → G8   G1 ← A6
   A3 → Y2   Y7 ← A6
       A3 → A6

O5 ← A6   A3 → O4
   G8 ← A6   A3 → G1
     Y2 ← A6   A3 → Y7
       Y2 → Y7

A6 → O5   O4 ← A3
   A6 → G8   G1 ← A3
     A6 → Y7   Y2 ← A3
       A6 → A3

Use the pattern above to make the apple-green arrowhead.

O5 → G8   G1 ← O4
    O5 → Y7   Y2 ← O4
O5 ← G8   G1 → O4
O5 → Y7   Y2 ← O4
    O5 → A3   A6 ← O4
      O5 → O4

G8 ← O4   O5 → G1
   Y7 ← O4   O5 → Y2
     A3 ← O4   O5 → A6
      A3 → A6

O4 → G8   G1 ← O5
  O4 → Y7   Y2 ← O5
    O4 → A6   A3 ← O5
     O4 → O5

Use this pattern to make the orange arrow-head and complete the design.

Completing the bracelet

At the end of the twenty-fourth row the order of colours is the same as at the beginning. However, the actual numerical order of threads will not be the same until the end of the forty-eighth row. Continue working the design from the first row until the bracelet reaches the required length. Separate the threads into two groups, plait a short length of each group and then tie them off in the usual way.

From the top: Leguana, Yanayacu and Chinajá.

Izalco

Nine threads are used to make this design rather than the usual eight or ten. Essentially the pattern is a V-shape with a six-row repeating pattern. The first four rows have two colours in each row while the fifth and sixth rows are solid colour and knotted with the central thread.

In this design half-knots are used to tie each half-row to the central thread. As the pattern progresses you should find that the V-shape made with the central thread protrudes beyond the straight edges of the other Vs.

You will need 1.6m (63in) lengths of four different coloured threads and a 1.1m (43in) length of a fifth colour. I have used pink (P1 and P2), green (G3 and G4), violet (V5), blue (B6 and B7) and fuchsia (F8 and F9).

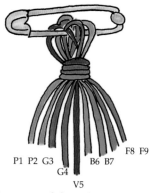

Fold the four equal lengths in half, add the fifth length and tie a knot. Attach a safety pin to the loop and arrange the threads in the order shown above.

row 1

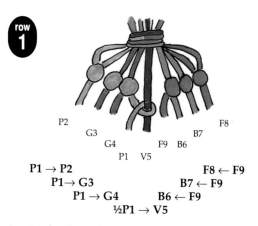

$$P1 \rightarrow P2 \qquad\qquad F8 \leftarrow F9$$
$$P1 \rightarrow G3 \qquad\qquad B7 \leftarrow F9$$
$$P1 \rightarrow G4 \qquad B6 \leftarrow F9$$
$$\tfrac{1}{2}P1 \rightarrow V5$$

1a. Make three forward knots with P1 around P2, G3 and G4. Make three backward knots with F9 around F8, B7 and B6. Make half a forward knot with P1 around V5.

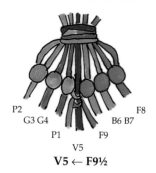

$$V5 \leftarrow F9\tfrac{1}{2}$$

1b. Now make half a backward knot with F9 around V5.

row 2

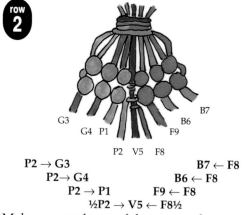

$$P2 \rightarrow G3 \qquad\qquad B7 \leftarrow F8$$
$$P2 \rightarrow G4 \qquad\qquad B6 \leftarrow F8$$
$$P2 \rightarrow P1 \qquad F9 \leftarrow F8$$
$$\tfrac{1}{2}P2 \rightarrow V5 \leftarrow F8\tfrac{1}{2}$$

Make a second row of the same colours using threads P2 and F8.

42

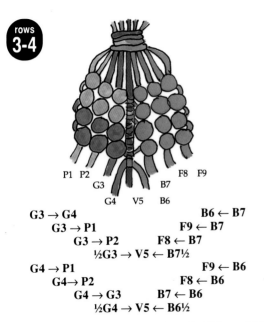

rows 3-4

P1 P2   F8 F9
        G3   B7
          G4   V5   B6

$$G3 \rightarrow G4 \qquad\qquad B6 \leftarrow B7$$
$$G3 \rightarrow P1 \qquad\qquad F9 \leftarrow B7$$
$$G3 \rightarrow P2 \qquad F8 \leftarrow B7$$
$$\tfrac{1}{2}G3 \rightarrow V5 \leftarrow B7\tfrac{1}{2}$$
$$G4 \rightarrow P1 \qquad\qquad F9 \leftarrow B6$$
$$G4 \rightarrow P2 \qquad F8 \leftarrow B6$$
$$G4 \rightarrow G3 \qquad B7 \leftarrow B6$$
$$\tfrac{1}{2}G4 \rightarrow V5 \leftarrow B6\tfrac{1}{2}$$

Using the green and blue threads (G3 and B7, and G4 and B6), make another two rows of knots in a similar way, using this pattern above.

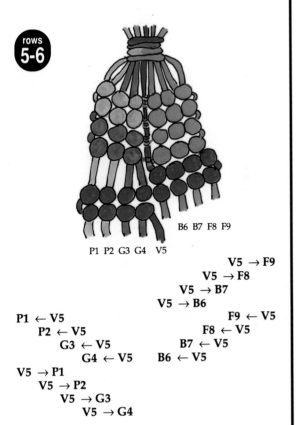

rows 5-6

                            B6 B7 F8 F9

P1 P2 G3 G4   V5

$$V5 \rightarrow F9$$
$$V5 \rightarrow F8$$
$$V5 \rightarrow B7$$
$$V5 \rightarrow B6$$
$$P1 \leftarrow V5 \qquad\qquad F9 \leftarrow V5$$
$$P2 \leftarrow V5 \qquad F8 \leftarrow V5$$
$$G3 \leftarrow V5 \qquad B7 \leftarrow V5$$
$$G4 \leftarrow V5 \quad B6 \leftarrow V5$$
$$V5 \rightarrow P1$$
$$V5 \rightarrow P2$$
$$V5 \rightarrow G3$$
$$V5 \rightarrow G4$$

Pick up V5 and, starting in the middle of the bracelet, make four forward knots working up the diagonal to the right.

Change to backward knots and make four knots with V5 back down the diagonal.

Now work up the other side of the V-shape with a further four backward knots. Take care to position the first of these knots up against the very first violet knot (in the diagram, these knots are shown away from those in the previous row in order to illustrate the sequence of knots).

Finally, change to forward knots and work back down to the middle of the bracelet to complete the double row of violet. Note that these two rows contain a total of eight knots compared to the six full knots and the two half-knots in the other rows.

Completing the bracelet

At the end of the sixth row the pattern is complete and the threads are in the same order as at the beginning. Continue the pattern of the first six rows until the bracelet reaches the required length. Separate the threads in to three groups, plait a short length and tie off with small knots.

Tehuacán

This rope-like bracelet is completely different from any of the preceding ones. It is worked basically as two groups of four threads which are then linked in the middle at the fifth and sixth rows with two half knots. The end result gives the impression of twisted multi-coloured ropes.

*You will need 1.7m (67in) lengths of four different coloured threads. I have used **red** (R1 and R2), **fuchsia** (F3 and F4), **violet** (V5 and V6) and **yellow** (Y7 and Y8).*

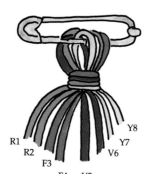

Fold the threads in half and prepare them in the usual way. Arrange the threads in the order shown above.

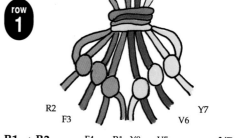

row 1

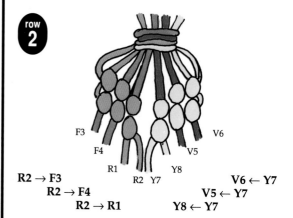

R2   F3   Y7   V6

R1 → R2   F4   R1 Y8 V5   Y7 ← Y8
  R1 → F3   V6 ← Y8
    R1 → F4   V5 ← Y8

Start at the outer edges and make three forward knots with thread R1 and three backward knots with thread Y8.

row 2

F3   V6
  F4   V5
    R1   Y8

R2 → F3   R2 Y7   V6 ← Y7
  R2 → F4   V5 ← Y7
    R2 → R1   Y8 ← Y7

Make a similar two half rows with threads R2 and Y7.

rows 3-4

R1   Y8
  R2   Y7
    F3   V5
      F4 V5

F3 → F4   V5 ← V6
  F3 → R1   Y8 ← V6
    F3 → R2   Y7 ← V6
F4 → R1   Y8 ← V5
  F4 → R2   Y7 ← V5
    F4 → F3   V6 ← V5

Repeat the pattern with two further sets of half rows with F3 and V6, and with F4 and V5.

44

row 5

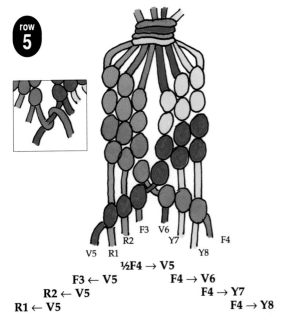

V5　R1　　　　　Y8
　　R2　F3　V6
　　　　　　Y7　　　　F4

½F4 → V5
F3 ← V5　　　　　F4 → V6
R2 ← V5　　　　　　　F4 → Y7
R1 ← V5　　　　　　　　　F4 → Y8

Make a half forward knot (see inset) with F4 around V5 and then continue with forward knots of F4 around V6, Y7 and Y8. Move back to the middle and complete the row with three backward knots of V5 around F3, R2 and R1.

row 6

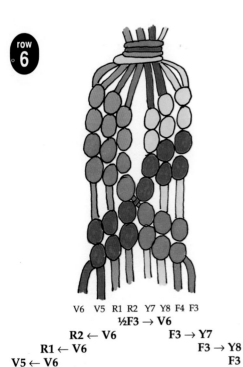

V6　V5　R1　R2　Y7　Y8　F4　F3
½F3 → V6
R2 ← V6　　　　　F3 → Y7
R1 ← V6　　　　　　　F3 → Y8
V5 ← V6　　　　　　　　　F3 → F4

Repeat the pattern of the fifth row, making a similar series of knots with F3 and V6. The basic design is now complete but the threads are in a different colour order from that at the start.

rows 7-12

V6 → V5	F4 ← F3
V6 → R1	Y8 ← F3
V6 → R2	Y7 ← F3
V5 → R1	Y8 ← F4
V5 → R2	Y7 ← F4
V5 → V6	F3 ← F4
R1 → R2	Y7 ← Y8
R1 → V6	F3 ← Y8
R1 → V5	F4 ← Y8
R2 → V6	F3 ← Y7
R2 → V5	F4 ← Y7
R2 → R1	Y8 ← Y7
½R2 → Y7	
R1 → Y7	R2 → Y8
V5 ← Y7	R2 → F4
V6 ← Y7	R2 → F3
½R1 → Y8	
V5 ← Y8	R1 → F4
V6 ← Y8	R1 → F3
Y7 ← Y8	R1 → R2

Make the series of knots shown above. At the end of the twelfth row the order of the threads is the reverse of that at the beginning.

rows 13-18

Y8 → Y7	R2 ← R1
Y8 → V6	F3 ← R1
Y8 → V5	F4 ← R1
Y7 → V6	F3 ← R2
Y7 → V5	F4 ← R2
Y7 → Y8	R1 ← R2
V6 → V5	F4 ← F3
V6 → Y8	R1 ← F3
V6 → Y7	R2 ← F3
V5 → Y8	R1 ← F4
V5 → Y7	R2 ← F4
V5 → V6	F3 ← F4
½V5 → F4	
V6 ← F4	V5 → F3
Y7 ← F4	V5 → R2
Y8 ← F4	V5 → R1
½V6 → F3	
Y7 ← F3	V6 → R2
Y8 ← F3	V6 → R1
F4 ← F3	V6 → V5

This series of knots produces rows of colours which are the reverse of those made in the first six rows.

rows 19-24

F3 → F4	V5 ← V6
F3 → Y8	R1 ← V6
F3 → Y7	R2 ← V6
F4 → Y8	R1 ← V5
F4 → Y7	R2 ← V5
F4 → F3	V6 ← V5
Y8 → Y7	R2 ← R1
Y8 → F3	V6 ← R1
Y8 → F4	V5 ← R1
Y7 → F3	V6 ← R2
Y7 → F4	V5 ← R2
Y7 → Y8	R1 ← R2
½Y7 → R2	
Y8 ← R2	Y7 → R1
F4 ← R2	Y7 → V5
F3 ← R2	Y7 → V6
½Y8 → R1	
F4 ← R1	Y8 → V5
F3 ← R1	Y8 → V6
R2 ← R1	Y8 → Y7

This series of knots produces rows of colours which are the reverse of those made in the seventh to twelfth rows. The last row completes the pattern and the threads are now in the same order as at the beginning.

Tehuacán and Bagazán.

Completing the bracelet

Repeat the pattern until the bracelet is long enough, then divide the threads into two groups. Plait a short length of each group and then tie off the ends with small knots.

Jacala

Twelve threads are used for this bracelet: six long ones and six short ones. The long threads are knotted to form a series of crosses on to a weft that is formed by the six short threads in the middle.

This is a very open type of knotting, so be very careful to place the knots so that they make a uniform pattern.

*You will need a 1.8m (71in) and a 1.3m (51in) length each of three different colours. The colours used for the diagrams are **violet** (V1 and V12, and V6 and V7), **orange** (O2 and O11, and O5 and O8) and **magenta** (M3 and M10, and M4 and M9); the latter pair of each colour are the short threads.*

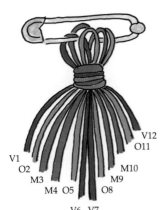

Fold each thread in half, tie a knot in the end, and prepare for work. Arrange the threads in the order shown above.

row 1

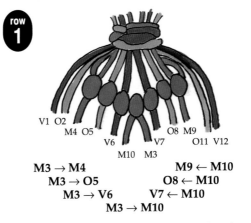

V1 O2   O8 M9
M4 O5   V6   V7   O11 V12
M10 M3

M3 → M4   M9 ← M10
M3 → O5   O8 ← M10
M3 → V6   V7 ← M10
M3 → M10

Ignore the outer two threads on each side and make three forward knots with M3 and three backward knots with M10. Slide the knots down to form a V-shape, then make a forward knot with M3 around M10.

row 2

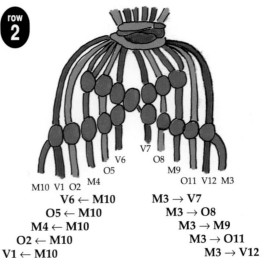

V7
V6   O8
O5   M9
M10 V1 O2 M4   O11 V12 M3
V6 ← M10   M3 → V7
O5 ← M10   M3 → O8
M4 ← M10   M3 → M9
O2 ← M10   M3 → O11
V1 ← M10   M3 → V12

Now make five backward knots with M10 and five forward knots with M3. Pull the knots down the weft to form the first cross of the design.

47

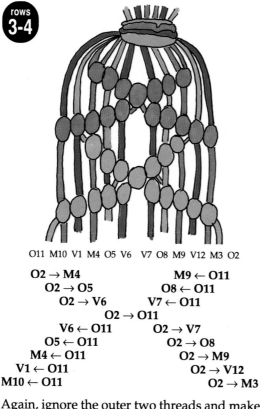

O11 M10 V1 M4 O5 V6   V7 O8 M9 V12 M3 O2

O2 → M4	M9 ← O11
O2 → O5	O8 ← O11
O2 → V6	V7 ← O11
O2 → O11	
V6 ← O11	O2 → V7
O5 ← O11	O2 → O8
M4 ← O11	O2 → M9
V1 ← O11	O2 → V12
M10 ← O11	O2 → M3

Again, ignore the outer two threads and make forward and backward knots with O2 and O11 to make the second cross.

rows 5-6

V1 → P4	O8 ← V12
V1 → O5	O8 ← V12
V1 → V6	V7 ← V12
V1 → V12	
V6 ← V12	V1 → V7
O5 ← V12	V1 → O8
P4 ← V12	V1 → P9
P10 ← V12	V1 → P3
O11 ← V12	V1 → O2

Now continue the pattern and make the third cross with the violet threads V1 and V12. At the end of the sixth row the arrangement of colours is the same as at the beginning, but although threads 4 to 9 are still in the same order, threads 1 to 3 and 10 to 12 are reversed.

rows 7-12

M10 → M4	M9 ← M3
M10 → O5	O8 ← M3
M10 → V6	V7 ← M3
M10 → M3	
V6 ← M3	M10 → V7
O5 ← M3	M10 → O8
M4 ← M3	M10 → M9
O11 ← M3	M10 → O2
V12 ← M3	M10 → V1
O11 → M4	M9 ← O2
O11 → O5	O8 ← O2
O11 → V6	V7 ← O2
O11 → O2	
V6 ← O2	O11 → V7
O5 ← O2	O11 → O8
M4 ← O2	O11 → M9
V12 ← O2	O11 → V1
M3 ← O2	O11 → M10
V12 → M4	M9 ← V1
V12 → O5	O8 ← V1
V12 → V6	V7 ← V1
V12 → V1	
V6 ← V1	V12 → V7
O5 ← V1	V12 → O8
M4 ← V1	V12 → M9
M3 ← V1	V12 → M10
O2 ← V1	V12 → O11

Make three more crosses in pink, orange and violet to complete the repeat sequence. At the end of the twelfth row the order of the threads is the same as at the beginning.

Completing the bracelet

Repeat the pattern from the first row until the bracelet is long enough. Divide the threads into four groups of three, plait a short length of each group and then tie a small knot in the end of each plait.

Azapa

The design of this bracelet is made from just two colours and features an openwork structure. You will have to position your knots with care in order to achieve a uniform pattern down the bracelet.

*To follow the pattern you will need four 1.8m (71in) lengths of **pink** (P1 to P4 and P7 to P10) and a single 1.8m (71in) length of **green** (G5 and G6).*

P1 P2 P3 P4 G5 G6 P7 P8 P9 P10

Prepare the threads in the usual way and arrange them in the order shown above.

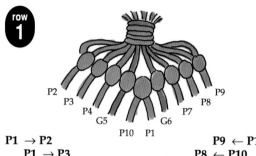

row 1

P1 → P2   P9 ← P10
  P1 → P3   P8 ← P10
    P1 → P4   P7 ← P10
      P1 → G5   G6 ← P10
        P1 → P10

Make four forward knots with P1 and four backward knots with P10, positioning the knots to form a V-shape. Make a forward knot with P1 around P10 to complete the row.

row 2

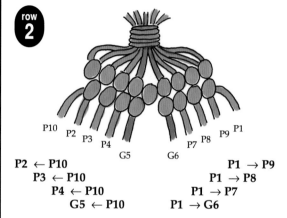

P2 ← P10   P1 → P9
  P3 ← P10   P1 → P8
    P4 ← P10   P1 → P7
      G5 ← P10   P1 → G6

Now move to the middle of the bracelet and make four backward knots with P10 and four forward knots with P1 to complete this row.

row 3

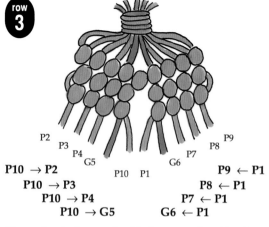

P10 → P2   P9 ← P1
  P10 → P3   P8 ← P1
    P10 → P4   P7 ← P1
      P10 → G5   G6 ← P1

Come back down the V-shape and make four forward knots with P10 and four backward knots with P1.

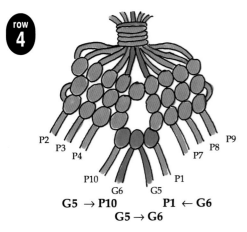

row 4

P2 P3 P4 P10 G6 G5 P1 P7 P8 P9

G5 → P10   P1 ← G6
G5 → G6

Make a small V-shape with G5 and G6.

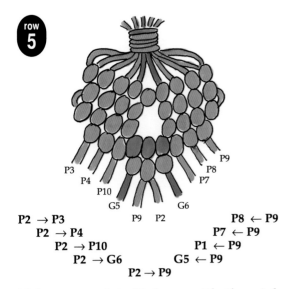

row 5

P3 P4 P10 G5 P9 P2 G6 P7 P8 P9

P2 → P3   P8 ← P9
 P2 → P4   P7 ← P9
  P2 → P10 P1 ← P9
   P2 → G6 G5 ← P9
    P2 → P9

Make a complete V-shape with the pink thread using forward knots with P2 and backward knots with P9.

rows 6-7

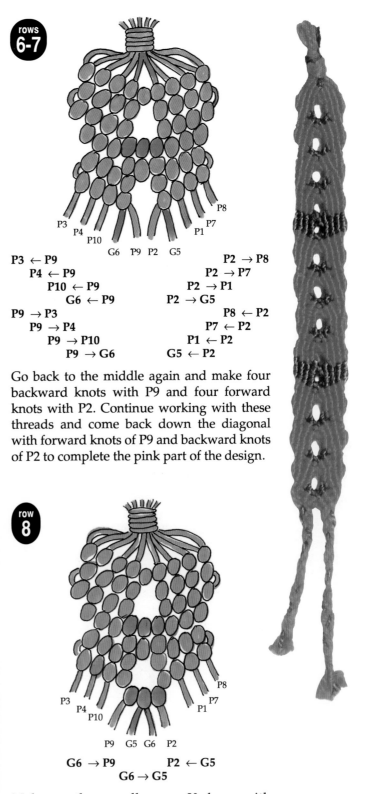

P3 P4 P10 G6 P9 P2 G5 P1 P7 P8

P3 ← P9   P2 → P8
 P4 ← P9   P2 → P7
  P10 ← P9   P2 → P1
   G6 ← P9 P2 → G5
P9 → P3   P8 ← P2
 P9 → P4   P7 ← P2
  P9 → P10   P1 ← P2
   P9 → G6 G5 ← P2

Go back to the middle again and make four backward knots with P9 and four forward knots with P2. Continue working with these threads and come back down the diagonal with forward knots of P9 and backward knots of P2 to complete the pink part of the design.

row 8

P3 P4 P10 P9 G5 G6 P2 P1 P7 P8

G6 → P9   P2 ← G5
G6 → G5

Make another small green V-shape with threads G6 and G5.

51

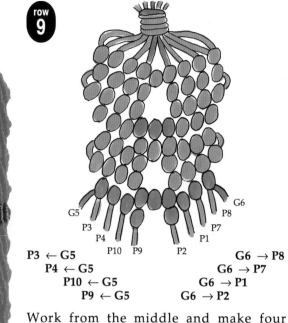

row 9

P3 ← G5	G6 → P8
P4 ← G5	G6 → P7
P10 ← G5	G6 → P1
P9 ← G5	G6 → P2

Work from the middle and make four backward knots with G5 and four forward knots with G6.

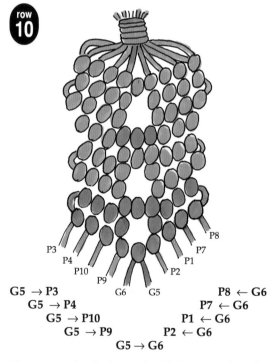

row 10

G5 → P3	P8 ← G6
G5 → P4	P7 ← G6
G5 → P10	P1 ← G6
G5 → P9	P2 ← G6
G5 → G6	

Now come back down the V-shape and make forward and backward knots with G5 and G6 to complete the pattern.

Completing the bracelet

At the end of the tenth row the threads are in the same colour order as at the beginning, but they are not in the same numerical order. In fact, they will not be in the same numerical order until the end of the fortieth row. However, continue the design by following the knots for the first ten rows and simply substitute numbers. When the bracelet reaches its final length, finish it off with two short lengths of plaiting and a couple of small knots.

Opposite. On the left arm, starting from the top: Taisha, Abunai, Azapa and Tehuacán. On the right arm, starting from the top: Cafifi, Jipijapa, Leguana and Tonosi.

Leguana

Diamonds are the theme of this design, which also includes short lengths of unknotted threads at the outer edges. As with the other more complex bracelets, take care to position the knots to make neat V- and inverted-V-shapes.

*Threads in a **mid green**, an **apple green**, a **yellow** and an **orange** are used to make this design. You will need two 1.6m (63in) lengths of one colour (in this example this is the darker green (G1, G3, G8 and G10)) and one 1.6m (63in) length each of three other colours (A2 and A9, Y4 and Y7, and O5 and O6).*

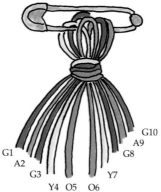

Prepare the threads in the normal way and arrange them in the order shown above.

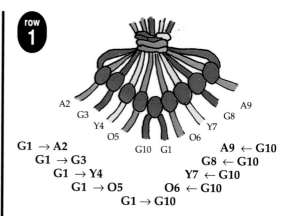

row 1

G1 → A2		A9 ← G10
G1 → G3		G8 ← G10
G1 → Y4		Y7 ← G10
G1 → O5		O6 ← G10
	G1 → G10	

Make forward and backward knots with G1 and G10, arranging the knots to form a good even V-shape.

rows 2-3

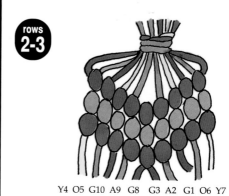

Y4 O5 G10 A9 G8 G3 A2 G1 O6 Y7

A2 → G3		G8 ← A9
A2 → Y4		Y7 ← A9
A2 → O5		O6 ← A9
A2 → G10	G1 ← A9	
	A2 → A9	
G3 → Y4		Y7 ← G8
G3 → O5		O6 ← G8
G3 → G10		G1 ← G8
G3 → A9	A2 ← G8	
	G3 → G8	

Make two more full rows of forward and backward knots using A2 and A9 and G3 and G8, positioning the knots tight up against the preceding row.

54

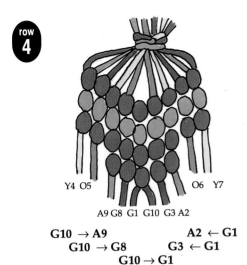

row 4

Y4 O5   O6 Y7

A9 G8 G1 G10 G3 A2

$$G10 \rightarrow A9 \qquad\qquad A2 \leftarrow G1$$
$$G10 \rightarrow G8 \qquad\quad G3 \leftarrow G1$$
$$G10 \rightarrow G1$$

Ignore the outer two threads on each side and make forward and backward knots with G10 and G1.

rows 5-6

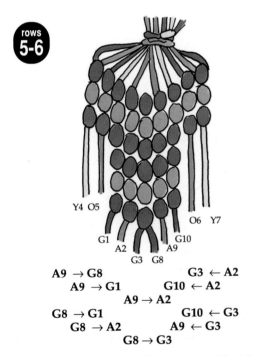

Y4 O5

O6 Y7

G1   G10

A2   A9

G3   G8

$$A9 \rightarrow G8 \qquad\qquad G3 \leftarrow A2$$
$$A9 \rightarrow G1 \qquad\quad G10 \leftarrow A2$$
$$A9 \rightarrow A2$$
$$G8 \rightarrow G1 \qquad\qquad G10 \leftarrow G3$$
$$G8 \rightarrow A2 \qquad\qquad A9 \leftarrow G3$$
$$G8 \rightarrow G3$$

Now make two more short rows with A9 and A2 and then G8 and G3.

row 7

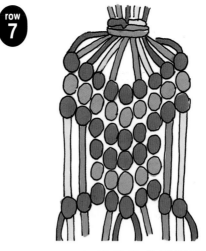

G1 Y4 O5 A2 G3 G8 A9 O6 Y7 G10

$$O5 \leftarrow G1 \qquad\qquad\qquad G10 \rightarrow O6$$
$$Y4 \leftarrow G1 \qquad\qquad\qquad G10 \rightarrow Y7$$

Make two backward knots with G1 around O5 and Y4 and two forward knots with G10 around O6 and Y7, positioning the knots to start the inverted V-shape.

rows 8-9

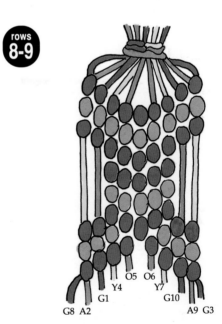

O5 O6

Y4   Y7

G1   G10

G8 A2   A9 G3

$$O5 \leftarrow A2 \qquad\qquad A9 \rightarrow O6$$
$$Y4 \leftarrow A2 \qquad\qquad A9 \rightarrow Y7$$
$$G1 \leftarrow A2 \qquad\qquad\quad A9 \rightarrow G10$$
$$O5 \leftarrow G8 \qquad\quad G3 \rightarrow O6$$
$$Y4 \leftarrow G8 \qquad\qquad G3 \rightarrow Y7$$
$$G1 \leftarrow G8 \qquad\qquad\quad G3 \rightarrow G3$$
$$A2 \leftarrow G8 \qquad\qquad\qquad G3 \rightarrow A9$$

Continue to build up the inverted V-shape with three and then four knots each of A2 and A9, and G8 and G3 respectively.

55

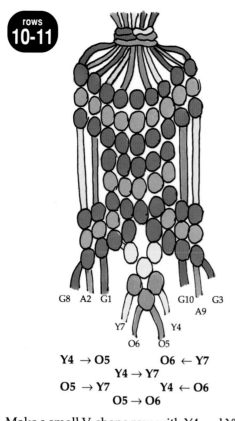

**rows
10-11**

G8 A2 G1   G10   G3
                          A9
        Y7   Y4
          O6   O5

Y4 → O5   O6 ← Y7
        Y4 → Y7
O5 → Y7   Y4 ← O6
        O5 → O6

Make a small V-shape row with Y4 and Y7 and
then a similar row with O5 and O6.

Completing the bracelet

At the end of the eleventh row the pattern is
complete and, although the actual numerical
order will not be the same until the forty-
fourth row, the order of colours is the same as
at the beginning. By now you should under-
stand how to continue with the design without
having to refer to a numbered pattern. Use the
pattern described for the first eleven rows to
repeat the design until the bracelet is the correct length. Finish the ends in the usual way.

*From left to right: Chinajá, Yanayacu and
Leguana; Tehuacán, Amaluza and Itatuba.*

Tucanao

Here we have a four-colour bracelet with a pattern that is very easy to follow, and that produces a multi-coloured W-shape down the length of the bracelet. The pattern consists of just two rows of knots, with the colour repeating every eight rows. However, the numerical order will not be the same as at the beginning until the end of the sixteenth row.

*Nice bright colours show off this design; you will want four 1.6m (63in) lengths of four different colours. I have used a **mid green** (G1 and G8), an **apple green** (A2 and A7), a **yellow** (Y3 and Y6) and a **red** (R4 and R5).*

G1 A2 Y3 R4   R5 Y6 A7 G8

Prepare as normal and arrange them in the order shown above.

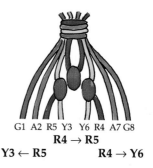

row 1

G1 A2 R5 Y3 Y6 R4 A7 G8

R4 → R5

Y3 ← R5   **R4 → Y6**

Start in the middle of the threads and make a forward knot with R4 around R5. Then make a backward knot with R5 around Y3 and a forward knot with R4 around Y6.

row 2

A2 R5 G1 Y3 Y6 G8 R4 A7

G1 → A2   **A7 ← G8**

G1 → R5   **R4 ← G8**

Move to the outer edges and make two forward knots with G1 and two backward knots with G8. These two rows produce the basic W-shape which is repeated in different colours down the bracelet.

row 3

A2 R5 Y6 G1 G8 Y3 R4 A7

Y3 → Y6

G1 ← Y6   **Y3 → G8**

Repeat the pattern of knots from row 1 with Y3 and Y6.

row 4

R5 Y6 A2 G1 G8 A7 Y3 R4

A2 → R5   R4 ← A7
   A2 → Y6   Y3 ← A7

Follow the pattern and complete the second W-shape with the apple-green threads A2 and A7.

rows 5-6

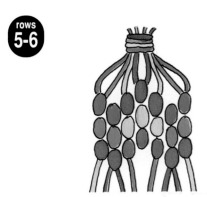

Y6 G8 R5 A2 A7 R4 G1 Y3
          G1 → G8
      A2 ← G8   G1 → A7
R5 → Y6   Y3 ← R4
   R5 → G8   G1 ← R4

Make a similar shape with the mid-green and red threads.

rows 7-8

G8 A7 Y6 R5 R4 Y3 A2 G1
         A2 → A7
     R5 ← A7   A2 → R4
Y6 → G8   G1 ← Y3
   Y6 → A7   A2 ← Y3

Now make a fourth W-shape with the apple-green and yellow threads to complete the repeating design.

Completing the bracelet

At the end of the eighth row the order of the colours will be the same as at the beginning of the bracelet, but the numerical order is reversed. Repeat the pattern (substituting the thread numbers accordingly) until you have reached the required length, separate the threads into two groups of four, plait each group and tie off with two small knots.

The Tucanao design made with a different set of coloured threads.

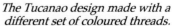

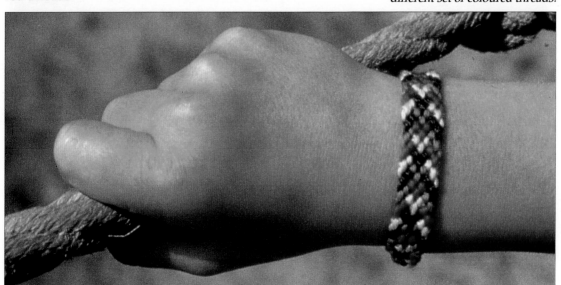

Ocotal

Here is another openwork bracelet using ten threads of five colours. The middle four threads act as a weft around which the knots are placed. The design is a series of interwoven crosses made up from the outer three threads on each side. As with other designs of this type it is very important to adjust the position of the knots at the end of each row.

*You will need 1.8m (71in) lengths of three colours and 0.8m (32in) lengths of two other colours. The shorter lengths are the weft around which the design is 'woven'. I have used **orange** (O1 and O10), **green** (G2 and G9), **blue** (B3 and B8), **lilac** (L4 and L7) and **yellow** (Y5 and Y6).*

O1 G2 B3 L4 Y5 Y6 L7 B8 G9 O10

Prepare the threads as usual and arrange them in the order shown above; the short threads are the lilac and the yellow. As the design progresses you will note that these four threads remain as straight strands through the bracelet.

row 1

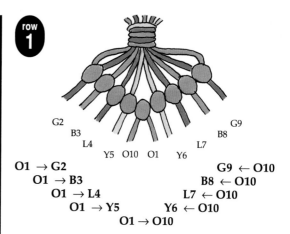

G2   G9
  B3   B8
    L4   L7
      Y5 O10 O1 Y6

O1 → G2   G9 ← O10
  O1 → B3   B8 ← O10
    O1 → L4   L7 ← O10
      O1 → Y5   Y6 ← O10
          O1 → O10

Make a half row of forward knots with O1 and another half row of backward knots with O10. Arrange the knots to form a shallow V-shape and then complete the row with a forward knot of O1 around O10.

row 2

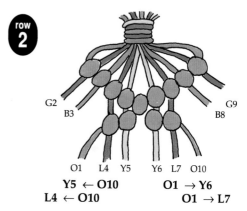

G2   G9
  B3   B8

      O1   L4 Y5   Y6 L7 O10
    Y5 ← O10   O1 → Y6
  L4 ← O10   O1 → L7

Make two backward knots with O10 and two forward knots with O1. Adjust the position of the knots so that they continue the angle of the V-shape in the first row to form a cross.

row 3

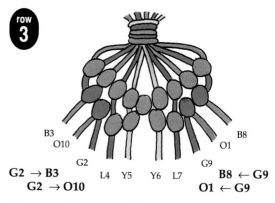

    B3   B8
      O10   O1
        G2   G9
G2 → B3   L4 Y5 Y6 L7   B8 ← G9
  G2 → O10   O1 ← G9

Move to the outer threads and make two forward knots with thread G2 and two backward knots with G9.

60

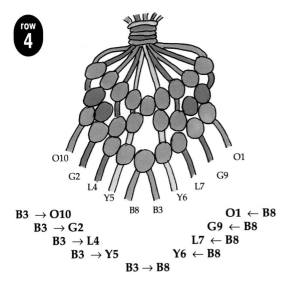

O10   O1
  G2   G9
    L4   L7
      Y5   Y6
           B8   B3

B3 → O10   **O1 ← B8**
  B3 → G2   **G9 ← B8**
    B3 → L4   **L7 ← B8**
      B3 → Y5   **Y6 ← B8**
           B3 → B8

Start the second cross with a full row of blue knots using threads B3 and B8.

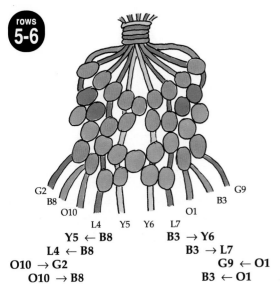

G2   G9
  B8   B3
    O10   O1
       L4   Y5   Y6   L7
         Y5 ← B8   **B3 → Y6**
       L4 ← B8   **B3 → L7**
O10 → G2   **G9 ← O1**
  O10 → B8   **B3 ← O1**

Complete the second cross with the blue threads, using the pattern of knots shown above.

G2 → B8   **B3 ← G9**
  G2 → O10   **O1 ← G9**
    G2 → L4   **L7 ← G9**
      G2 → Y5   **Y6 ← G9**
           G2 → G9
      Y5 ← G9   **G2 → Y6**
    L4 ← G9   **G2 → L7**
B8 → O10   **O1 ← B3**
  B8 → G9   **G2 ← B3**

Now make the third cross using the green threads G2 and G9 and complete the pattern with two forward knots with B8 and two backward knots with B3.

Completing the bracelet

At the end of the ninth row the colours are in the same order as at the beginning but the actual numerical order will not be the same until the end of the eighteenth row. Continue the pattern of the first nine rows, substituting the numbers as appropriate until the bracelet is the required length. Finish off the end in the usual way.

Tarata (top) and Ocotal (bottom).

Tonosi

This last bracelet is made with twelve threads and is one of the widest of the designs in this book. The repeating diamond pattern in two strong colours stands out from the backgoround of two paler colours. The centre of the large diamond is left open with just a weft of the paler threads visible. As it is an openwork design, be careful to place the knots correctly, especially when forming the large diamond shapes.

You will need a 1.6m (63in) length of each of the two pale colours and a 2.1m (83in) length of each of the darker ones. The threads used for this example are green (G1 to G4), blue (B5 and B8), ultramarine blue (U6 and U7) and yellow (Y9 to Y12).

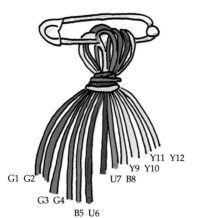

Prepare the threads and then arrange them in two groups as shown in the diagram above.

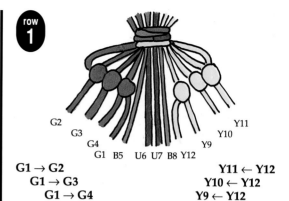

row 1

G1 → G2	Y11 ← Y12
G1 → G3	Y10 ← Y12
G1 → G4	Y9 ← Y12

Working from the outer edges, make three forward knots with G1 and three backward knots with Y12.

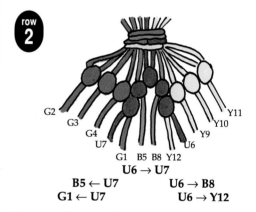

row 2

U6 → U7	
B5 ← U7	U6 → B8
G1 ← U7	U6 → Y12

Move to the middle and make a forward knot with U6 around U7. Now make two backward knots with U7 and two forward knots with U6. Place these four knots to form a small inverted V-shape.

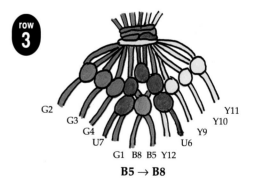

row 3

B5 → B8

Go back to the middle and make a forward knot with B5 around B8. This fills in the centre of what will become the small diamond.

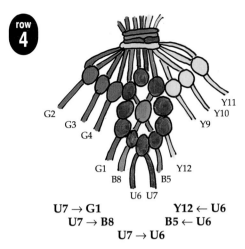

row 4

U7 → G1   Y12 ← U6
U7 → B8   B5 ← U6
          U7 → U6

Now bring the ultramarine threads back into the middle with forward and backward knots to complete the small diamond.

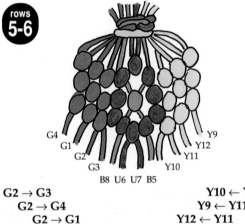

rows 5-6

G2 → G3   Y10 ← Y11
G2 → G4   Y9 ← Y11
  G2 → G1   Y12 ← Y11
G3 → G4   Y9 ← Y10
  G3 → G1   Y12 ← Y10
    G3 → G2   Y11 ← Y10

Go back to the outer edges and make forward knots with the green threads G2 and G3 and backward knots with the yellow threads Y11 and Y12 to form the background area of the design.

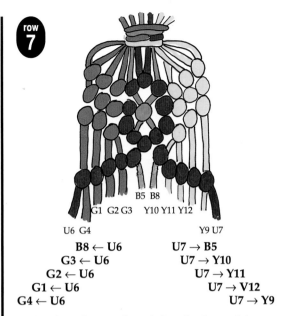

row 7

B8 ← U6   U7 → B5
G3 ← U6   U7 → Y10
G2 ← U6   U7 → Y11
G1 ← U6   U7 → V12
G4 ← U6   U7 → Y9

Make five forward and five backward knots with U6 and U7, positioning the knots at the same angle as the bottom sides of the small diamond.

row 8

          B8 → B5
G3 ← B5   B8 → Y10
G2 ← B5   B8 → Y11
G1 ← B5   B8 → Y12
G4 ← B5   B8 → Y9
U6 ← B5   B8 → U7

Make a forward knot with B8 around B5 and then make five backward and five forward knots with B5 and B8 following the angle of the previous row.

63

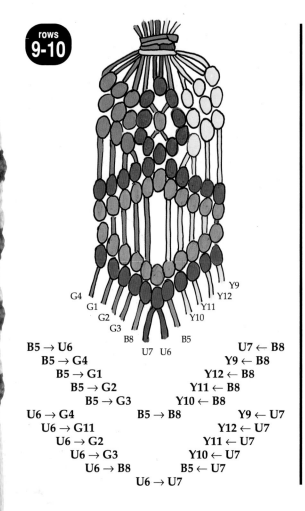

rows 9-10

G4
G1
G2
G3
B8   B5
U7 U6

Y9
Y12
Y11
Y10

B5 → U6	U7 ← B8
B5 → G4	Y9 ← B8
B5 → G1	Y12 ← B8
B5 → G2	Y11 ← B8
B5 → G3	Y10 ← B8
U6 → G4	B5 → B8	Y9 ← U7
U6 → G11	Y12 ← U7
U6 → G2	Y11 ← U7
U6 → G3	Y10 ← U7
U6 → B8	B5 ← U7
U6 → U7	

Complete the inner border of the large diamond; make a series of five forward knots with B5 and five backward knots with B8. Position the knots by sliding them down the weft of threads to form a good diamond. Make a forward knot with B5 around B8 to finish the diamond.

Now make the outer border of the large diamond. Make five forward knots with U6 and five backward knots with U7. At this stage the whole pattern has been developed and the threads are back in the same colour order as at the beginning.

Completing the bracelet

Note that the last knot in row 10 (U6 around U7) is equivalent to the first knot of the second row of the pattern. Repeat the ten-row pattern. The colour references are correct but the numerical order will not be the same as at the start until the end of the fortieth row. When the bracelet is long enough, separate the threads into four groups of three, plait a short length of each group and tie off the ends with a small knot.

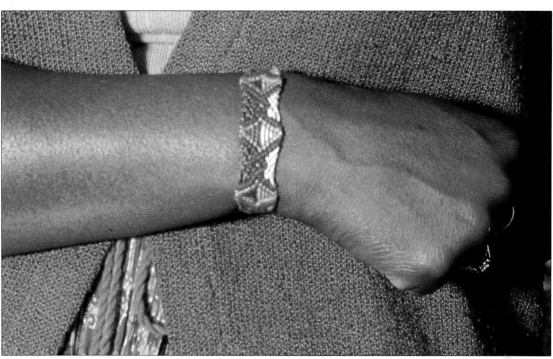